Management Extra

PROJECT MANAGEMENT

Management Extra
PROJECT MANAGEMENT

ELSEVIER

eLEARN

Pergamon
Flexible
Learning

AMSTERDAM • BOSTON • HEIDELBERG • LONDON • NEW YORK • OXFORD • PARIS •
SAN DIEGO • SAN FRANCISCO • SINGAPORE • SYDNEY • TOKYO

Pergamon Flexible Learning is an imprint of Elsevier
Linacre House, Jordan Hill, Oxford OX2 8DP
30 Corporate Drive, Burlington, MA 01803

First published 2005
Revised edition 2007

© 2007 Wordwide Learning Limited adapted by Elearn Limited
Published by Elsevier Ltd
All rights reserved

No part of this publication may be reproduced, stored in a retrieval system or transmitted in any form or by any means electronic, mechanical, photocopying, recording or otherwise without the prior written permission of the publisher

Permissions may be sought directly from Elsevier's Science & Technology Rights Department in Oxford, UK: phone (+44) (0) 1865 843830; fax (+44) (0) 1865 853333; email: permissions@elsevier.com. Alternatively you can submit your request online by visiting the Elsevier web site at http://elsevier.com/locate/permissions, and selecting *Obtaining permission to use Elsevier material*

Notice
No responsibility is assumed by the publisher for any injury and/or damage to persons or property as a matter of products liability, negligence or otherwise, or from any use or operation of any methods, products, instructions or ideas contained in the material herein.

British Library Cataloguing in Publication Data
A catalogue record for this book is available from the British Library

Library of Congress Cataloging-in-Publication Data
A catalog record for this book is available from the Library of Congress

ISBN: 978-0-080-48989-6

For information on all Pergamon Flexible Learning publications visit our web site at books.elsevier.com

Printed and bound in Italy

Working together to grow
libraries in developing countries

www.elsevier.com | www.bookaid.org | www.sabre.org

ELSEVIER   BOOK AID International   Sabre Foundation

Contents

List of activities	vii
List of figures	viii
List of tables	ix
Series preface	xi
Introduction: managing successful projects	xiii

1 What is a project? — 1
- The characteristics of a project? — 1
- The project life cycle — 5
- Recap — 11
- More @ — 12

2 Project initiation and definition — 13
- Project roles and responsibilities — 13
- Testing feasibility — 18
- Agreeing the vision and objectives — 21
- Scope, constraints and deliverables — 27
- Risk analysis and contingency planning — 31
- Recap — 37
- More @ — 38

3 Project planning — 39
- Team roles — 39
- Work breakdown structure and task definition — 49
- Resource plan and commitment matrix — 53
- Project network techniques — 56
- Gantt charts — 64
- Recap — 68
- More @ — 69

4 Putting the plan into action — 70
- Qualities of the project manager — 70
- Building and motivating the team — 78
- Project progress and review — 83
- Dealing with problems — 88
- Recap — 94
- More @ — 95

5 Project completion — 96
- Project completion, sign off and review — 96
- Recap — 100
- More @ — 101

References — 102

Activities

Activity 1	Identify the characteristics of projects	4
Activity 2	Define key activities	9
Activity 3	Develop an idea for your own project	10
Activity 4	Explore the role of stakeholders	16
Activity 5	Carry out a forcefield analysis	20
Activity 6	Evaluate SMART objectives	24
Activity 7	Devise SMART objectives	25
Activity 8	Conduct a risk analysis	34
Activity 9	Prepare a project Terms of Reference	36
Activity 10	Identify your preferred team role	42
Activity 11	Prepare a Work Breakdown Structure	51
Activity 12	Construct an Activity on Arrow diagram	62
Activity 13	Prepare a Gantt chart	65
Activity 14	Assess your project management skills	76
Activity 15	Identify the stages of team development	81
Activity 16	Explore the Nominal Group Technique	93
Activity 17	Analyse strengths and weaknesses of a project	99

Figures

1.1	Project stages	5
2.1	Forcefield analysis on the introduction of online trading	19
2.2	Creating a vision statement	22
2.3	The probability of achieving a successful outcome – home extension project	33
3.1	Part of a Work Breakdown Structure	49
3.2	Considering key resources	53
3.3	Using AoA diagrams (1)	58
3.4	Using AoA diagrams (2)	58
3.5	Using AoA diagrams (3)	58
3.6	Using AoA diagrams (4)	58
3.7	Tea time	59
3.8	Using dummy activities	59
3.9	Showing time	59
3.10	AoA network for project to improve delivery times	60
3.11	Using AoN diagrams (1)	60
3.12	Using AoN diagrams (2)	60
3.13	Using AoN diagrams (3)	61
3.14	Using AoN diagrams (4)	61
3.15	Using AoN diagrams (5)	61
3.16	AoN network	61
3.17	AoN network for project to improve delivery times	62
3.18	Gantt chart	64
4.1	The team development clock	78
4.2	The monitoring process	83
4.3	The project 'S' curve representation	86
4.4	Fishbone diagram	89
4.5	The PDCA cycle	90

Tables

2.1	Key stakeholders and roles	14
3.1	Belbin's team role types	40
3.2	Commitment matrix	56

Series preface

Whether you are a tutor/trainer or studying management development to further your career, Management Extra provides an exciting and flexible resource helping you to achieve your goals. The series is completely new and up-to-date, and has been written to harmonise with the 2004 national occupational standards in management and leadership. It has also been mapped to management qualifications, including the Institute of Leadership & Management's middle and senior management qualifications at Levels 5 and 7 respectively on the revised national framework.

For learners, coping with all the pressures of today's world, Management Extra offers you the flexibility to study at your own pace to fit around your professional and other commitments. Suddenly, you don't need a PC or to attend classes at a specific time – choose when and where to study to suit yourself! And, you will always have the complete workbook as a quick reference just when you need it.

For tutors/trainers, Management Extra provides an invaluable guide to what needs to be covered, and in what depth. It also allows learners who miss occasional sessions to 'catch up' by dipping into the series.

This series provides unrivalled support for all those involved in management development at middle and senior levels.

Reviews of Management Extra

I have utilised the Management Extra series for a number of Institute of Leadership and Management (ILM) Diploma in Management programmes. The series provides course tutors with the flexibility to run programmes in a variety of formats, from fully facilitated, using a choice of the titles as supporting information, to a tutorial based programme, where the complete series is provided for home study. These options also give course participants the flexibility to study in a manner which suits their personal circumstances. The content is interesting, thought provoking and up-to-date, and, as such, I would highly recommend the use of this series to suit a variety of individual and business needs.

Martin Davies BSc(Hons) MEd CEngMIMechE MCIPD FITOL FInstLM
Senior Lecturer, University of Wolverhampton Business School

At last, the complete set of books that make it all so clear and easy to follow for tutor and student. A must for all those taking middle/senior management training seriously.

Michael Crothers, ILM National Manager

Managing successful projects

This book focuses on the activities involved in initiating, planning, implementing and completing a project successfully. In short, the activities associated with the term, 'project management'.

For simplicity, they are covered as if they follow a sequence of neatly compartmentalised activities that succeed each other in some pre-ordained order. In practice, life is much messier. It is a sequence of cycles, not a group of activities. Objectives, targets, plans and budgets are continually subject to review and revision to ensure that they still have a business rationale. Project outcomes often diverge considerably from the original draft plan.

The ideas you will find in this book can be applied to a wide range of projects that vary in size, complexity, cost and timescale. They are intended to be practical, to help you foresee potential problems and when they arise, to address them effectively. As well as covering the tools and techniques of project management, we also pay attention to the soft issues involved – how to manage the people side of project management.

The book is organised into five main themes. The first explores the fundamental characteristics of a project and the stages of its life cycle. The other four then look in detail at each of the life cycle steps.

Your objectives are to:

- Explore what differentiates a project from other types of work and identify the essential stages in the project life cycle
- Define the vision, objectives and scope of a project with the project sponsors and key stakeholders
- Identify the key elements of a project plan and practise network analysis techniques for project planning
- Learn how to identify and manage potential risks in relation to the project
- Find out what is involved in leading and monitoring a project effectively
- Explore how to bring a project to a close, evaluate its success and capture learning points for the future.

1 What is a project?

What makes a project a project?

A project involves using exactly the same skills that you use in everyday, routine work – planning, working alongside others, managing a variety of resources, reporting and so on.

It isn't defined by its size because this can vary enormously. Furthermore, it would seem that there is little similarity between a project to replace the office furniture, which will take two months, and a project to build a six-lane road bridge across a major river, which will take two years.

However, all projects, as you will explore in this first theme, do share common characteristics and have the same life cycle.

You will:

- **Identify the differences between a project and routine work**
- **Consider the work of the project manager**
- **Consider the different stages of the project life cycle.**

The characteristics a project

Let's begin with a definition of what a project is:

> A project is a temporary endeavour involving a connected sequence of activities and a range of resources, which is designed to achieve a specific and unique outcome, which operates within time, cost and quality constraints and which is often used to introduce change.

Source: *Lake* (1997)

To take the key points one by one:

- It is **temporary**: it has a clearly defined and agreed start and finish date.
- It involves a **connected sequence of activities**: however short and localised, or long and complex, a project will have a specific set of activities that are linked together and interdependent.
- It requires a **range of resources**: all projects will have a quantified and dedicated resource requirement, such as

> people, systems, space, time, or specialist or expert external input.
>
> ◆ It has a **specific and unique outcome**, which can be evaluated: each project's aims and objectives will be different and unique to that project.
>
> ◆ It **introduces change**: a project is often used as an instrument for change. As a result of it, differences may be expected in the way people work, communicate or go about their daily lives.

Projects can cover many different types of activity. For example, they can investigate a specific problem, research a new product or service, or be set up to implement the findings of an earlier project. They can be carried out entirely in-house by an organisation's own staff, make use of external consultants, involve several companies working together in a consortium, or any mix of these.

Conventional routine work, on the other hand, tends to be a series of known and recurring tasks, which have no clearly defined end point or deliverables, and tend to be carried out within a fairly stable environment – often within a single function.

When we call work 'a project' we are implying that it has a unique outcome, which can be evaluated in terms of time, cost and quality. For example, it would be appropriate to call building and launching London's Millennium Dome a project, and putting a man on the moon was obviously a project.

So projects vary in size but have in common this idea of a series of activities, which are planned and co-ordinated in such a way that a client or sponsor can eventually make a judgement as to whether or not they have received value for their investment.

> Was the Millennium Dome project, for example, value for money? What criteria should be used to make this judgement? Managing that project, even with all of the brilliance of architects, contractors, managers and consultants, still proved very difficult and for many produced an unsatisfactory outcome. Not least was the issue of when the dome project was actually complete. Was it when the doors were opened for the first visitor or when the end of year accounting, which showed a loss, was completed?

The project manager

The work of some organisations is based around projects – construction, advertising, consultancy or entertainment. In other organisations the work is centred on ongoing operations, such as manufacturing, distribution and travel. However, projects are increasingly used in all organisations, both to respond to changing circumstances and to create change.

Whatever the industry context in which you work, you are likely to become involved in managing projects at some time. For example, you may be asked to organise and implement a new layout for the office, to investigate and write a report on how to introduce new updated machinery, to organise the next sales conference in Paris or to evaluate and improve the provision of customer services. Your approach will be influenced by the organisational structure, and how projects within it are agreed and resourced.

> **The workplace of the future is going to be organized according to jobs that need doing. And that means a project-oriented workplace.**
> **Campbell (1995)**

However, to be successful as a project manager, you need to be quite clear about what it is that you have been charged to deliver, at what cost, to what performance standards, to whose satisfaction and by when. Additional considerations include what control you have over resources and people, and how certain you can be that the project that you have accepted is feasible within the constraints that define the sphere of operation.

Project management has spawned a host of tools and techniques for defining, setting up and controlling the work that has to be done. The tools can make the job easier, but a project can't be managed by numbers. Project managers must be superb at managing people, and at handling uncertainty and risk. It's not surprising then that experienced project managers of complex projects get paid a lot of money.

Discipline is a byword. Another is flexibility. Like grasping a bar of soap or trying to blow the perfect soap bubble, too much discipline can spell failure. The ability to apply a tight and yet loose approach is the hallmark of a skilled project manager.

Project Management

Activity 1
Identify the characteristics of projects

Objective

Use this activity to check your understanding of the characteristics of projects.

Task

1 Reflect on a recent project that has been or is being managed in your organisation.

2 Using the key characteristics of projects outlined in the chart below, assess how closely the project matches these characteristics.

3 Which of the five characteristics have proved difficult to manage and why do you think this has occurred?

4 In the light of your analysis, what conclusions can you draw about the way in which projects are defined within your organisation? Note down your thoughts below:

The project was or had:	Yes	No	Difficult to manage? Why?
Temporary	☐	☐	
A connected sequence of activities	☐	☐	
Dedicated resources	☐	☐	
A specific and unique outcome	☐	☐	
An instrument for change	☐	☐	

Your thoughts:

1 What is a project?

The project life cycle

Projects pass through some well-defined stages on their journey from initial idea to completion and sign off. There are basically five of these, as shown in Figure 1.1.

```
Initiation and definition
        ↓
Planning and project organisation
        ↓
Implementing the plan
        ↓
Monitoring and review
        ↓
Closure and evaluation
```

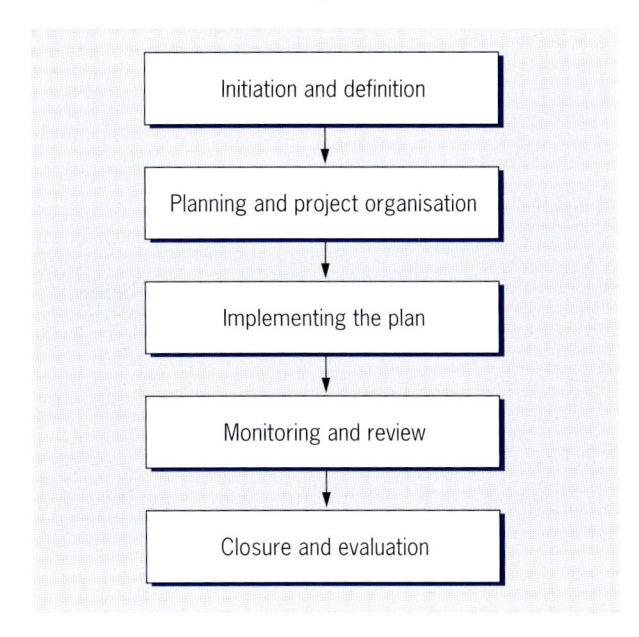

Figure 1.1 *Project stages*

Although each stage has a clear purpose, they are rarely as neatly compartmentalised as the model in Figure 1.1; stages may overlap. Monitoring and review, for instance, is inseparable from putting the plan into practice and the activities within each stage may continue to the next stage. The project manager needs to be aware of this, accept it as a part of real life, and be confident enough to manage this fluidity without losing control of the project.

All the stages are important, but it is wise to place particular emphasis on initiation and definition and the planning and project organisation phases. If these are skimmed over in a rush to get started on what may be perceived as the real work, implementation will be difficult and time-consuming to achieve, and the project will probably fail.

In his book *The Seven Habits of Highly Effective People,* author Steven Covey (1992) highlights the importance of early planning stages.

> All things are created twice. There's a mental or first creation, and a physical or second creation of all things. You have to make sure that the blueprint, the first creation, is really what you want; that you've thought everything through. Then you put it into bricks and mortar. Each day you go to the construction shed and pull out the blueprint to get marching orders for the day. You begin with the end in mind.

Source: *Covey* (1992)

As the project manager, you are in the spotlight, but projects involve many different people, all of whom have some interest in its progress and outcome.

These stakeholders include the project sponsor, who may have initiated the project, the customer or client for whom the work is being done, project team members, suppliers of products or services for the project, both internal and external, and possibly external consultants.

We will now look briefly at each stage in turn.

Initiation and definition

Projects can arise from a number of different sources, for different reasons. For example:

- a request from a potential customer to provide a service or product
- a customer complaint about poor delivery times
- an internal proposal for a new product or service
- your boss's view that there must be a better way of doing something
- your own belief that a particular process isn't working as efficiently as it should
- a policy decision in the organisation to introduce a new quality standard.

Large capital projects, for example civil engineering projects, are typically preceded by an extensive feasibility study. This study would have concluded that the project is viable, estimated the budget required, confirmed that the organisation can support the capital outlay and set out a broad specification for the project.

Some examples of this kind of feasibility study include:

- The best methods of converting paper media, in a documentation centre, into electronic versions suitable for the organisation's project work
- A study to define the technical and financial requirements of an improved environmental monitoring system in a major city
- Identifying businesses that need the particular attributes of a specific city or region, for example transport links, climate or raw materials, so that the city or region can use targeted marketing to encourage relocation.

Smaller but complex projects, those for which the value isn't immediately obvious or for which an initial quantification is required, can also benefit from feasibility or scoping study. This can establish a project framework and definition, and provide a clear view of what needs to be done by the project itself. This study will commonly have some formal recommendations for action or change. At the smaller end of the scale, projects may simply start as a gut feeling or hunch, which is then articulated into a project proposal.

The key document from the initiation and definition phase will be the terms of reference. This can present itself in a variety of ways. In its most recognisable form it is simply described as the project Terms of Reference. However, the feasibility or scoping study, or a project proposal, can equally well serve as the terms of reference, or project brief under which the project is to be carried out.

It may be helpful to think of it as the contract between the sponsor and the project team, which defines the scope of the work to be carried out. It can be initiated by either side, but the activities it covers, and any subsequent changes, have to be agreed by both parties.

The Terms of Reference will cover at least the following:

- the project sponsor
- the customer
- objectives, scope and budget for the project
- the kind of deliverables expected from it
- the different phases of the project and any milestones or key interim points that the project is looking to achieve.

At this stage, you may be working on your own as the project manager, or with a small number of people who will develop into the core project team.

You will cover terms of reference in more detail when you look at project initiation later in this book.

Project planning and organisation

This is a crucial and very extensive stage, which involves all the project's stakeholders, that is, everyone who has a legitimate interest in it. This is where the project really begins to move from an idea to a reality, as project outlines are translated into specific actions. The focus in this phase will be clarification, quantification and documentation, all of which will build up into a formal project plan:

Project Management

> - What tasks will be carried out in order to meet the project objectives and how will they be grouped together?
> - Who will be responsible for carrying them out?
> - What resources will be required?
> - In what order will tasks be performed, and to what timetable?

This phase of the project may well determine its success or failure. A key task for the project manager during this phase is obtaining agreement. It is essential that all project stakeholders believe in it and are committed to its success.

Implementing the plan

This is when it all becomes real, when you have to go away and do it. The success or failure of the project will depend to a large extent on how well the project team works together, and how effectively you can lead and motivate them. The project's customer – the person or group who will derive benefit from it – will be taking a close interest, and you must ensure that they are consulted as appropriate and kept up to date with progress.

Monitoring and review

If the project is to achieve its objectives against time and budget, it will need to be carefully monitored against the key dates and milestones you have identified in the project plan. Few projects run without any hitches, and you and your team will need to review the plan on a regular basis, deal with potential and actual problems, and make any necessary changes to the plan.

Project closure and evaluation

This signals the end of the project, when all deliverables can be formally signed off and the team disbanded. It is also the point at which the project itself can be evaluated in terms of its success and likely impact.

> **Summary of project stages**
> **Initiation** – what is the vision?
> **Planning** – how will the vision be achieved, by whom, by when and at what cost?
> **Implementation** – doing it!
> **Monitoring and review** – how well are you doing it?
> **Project closure and evaluation** – the vision made real, accepted, signed off and evaluated.

Activity 2
Define key activities

Objective
Use this activity to define the key activities of a project within your organisation.

Task
1 Select a project that you have been involved in or affected by during the past year.
2 Identify what the different stages were, and approximately how long each lasted.
3 Note down the key activities of each stage.

Project title:

Stage	Length of time involved	Key activities

Feedback

Some of the things you may like to consider from your analysis are:

- How long was the planning stage, in relation to the implementation stage? Taking too long or too short a time over planning can both indicate problems.
- Were the stages clearly defined? Paper plans are one thing, but reality is another, and the lines between different stages can be blurred.

Activity 3
Develop an idea for your own project

Objective

Use this activity to develop an idea for a project that you would like to carry out in your own field of work.

You will be asked to plan this project in the activities in this book. You can also use these activities as tools for your own work-based projects in the future.

There are broadly two types of work-based project you can carry out:

- A consultation project – here you analyse a problem, situation, challenge or opportunity related to your work, draw conclusions and recommend appropriate solutions, explaining how your solutions could be implemented.
- A change project – where you identify improvements to processes for which you have responsibility, and then implement appropriate changes to bring about particular benefits, such as cost savings or better customer service.

Task

1. Identify, on a separate sheet of paper, a project that you would like to carry out in your particular field. It could be either a consultation project or a change project.

    Factors to consider in selecting an appropriate project:
    - What problems and opportunities are you facing at work?
    - What processes in your work area are creating barriers or impeding the quality of the services or products you and your department provide to others?
    - What aspects of your work are you particularly interested in?

1 What is a project?

> - What are the views of your line manager?
> - How much time and other resources do you have, given your other work commitments?
> - Do you think your project is feasible?
>
> 2 When you have some project ideas, you may find it helpful to talk them through with your manager, and ask him or her to act as the project sponsor as you plan the project.

◆ Recap

Identify the differences between a project and routine work

- A project differs from routine work in that it has a defined start and end point, and involves a connected sequence of activities and a set of resources to achieve a specific and unique outcome or change.
- Projects can be characterised by their complexity and level of risk.

Consider the work of the project manager

- Project management is the process of managing the project activities by planning and executing the work, and by co-ordinating the contribution of the project team, to achieve the project outcomes to agreed quality levels, budget and timescales.
- In addition to managing project activities, project managers must be superb at managing people and at handling uncertainty and risk.

Consider the different stages of the project life cycle

- Project management has five stages:
  - Initiation and definition: What will the project achieve and is it feasible?
  - Planning and organisation: Focusing on clarification, quantification and documentation to build a formal project plan.
  - Implementation: Putting the plan into action.
  - Monitoring and review: Are key dates and milestones being achieved and are changes necessary?
  - Closure and evaluation: Signing off and evaluating to assess the project's success and impact and to extract learning points for the future.

▶▶ More @

Bruce, A. and Langdon, K. (2000) *Project Management,* Dorling Kindersley
This book offers 101 power tips on project management to help the reader handle real-life situations.

Lewis, J. (1999) *The Project Manager's Desk Reference*, McGraw-Hill
This widely acknowledged reference book is written for managers who wish to get deeper into project management tools and techniques.

Lientz, B. and Rea, K. (1998) *Project Management for the 21st Century,* Academic Press
Another more detailed text covering issues of project management organisation, process and technology, and exploring how modern technology tools can support effective project management and project success.

The Project Management Institute (PMI) – www.pmi.org
The *Project Management Body of Knowledge* is available as a download. It also offers:

- a collection of published articles and papers from 1990 to the present, all of which are abstracted and indexed electronically in the Knowledgebase.

- selected articles from *PM Network Online,* the official magazine of the PMI.

2 Project initiation and definition

This is the first phase in any project. Your aim is to develop a specification, or terms of reference, that sets out the size, scope and complexity of the project.

The Terms of Reference document answers four questions:

- **What is this project about?** Successful projects result from having a clear vision of how the project adds value to the organisation, customer or stakeholder group and well-defined objectives that describe the scope of the project.

- **How will the project be delivered?** You will outline the broad phases of the project, and the milestones or key interim points that will mark progress, and the resources that are required.

- **Is the project feasible?** No project has an unlimited budget or infinite timescales. You need to know the constraints within which your project will operate and the risks that impact its likelihood of success to determine whether it is feasible.

- **Is the project worthwhile?** There must be some recognisable benefit relative to the resources of time, money and effort invested by the project team.

These all need to be defined and agreed with the customer, the project sponsor and any other important stakeholders.

In this theme you look at project initiation and definition in more detail. Specifically, you will explore how to:

- Identify the key stakeholder groups and consider their likely role in a project
- Use a forcefield analysis to test the feasibility of a project
- Agree a vision and set objectives and key milestones for a project
- Set the scope for a project
- Identify and manage potential risks in relation to the project.

Project roles and responsibilities

Bringing a project to a successful conclusion will depend to a large extent on the goodwill, commitment and co-operation of many different people – these are your project stakeholders. Table 2.1 demonstrates the roles and responsibilities of these key stakeholder groups.

Stakeholder	Role
Customer Internal or external person or group who will benefit from the changes brought about by the project	– sets out the objectives of the project and states how its success is measured and how and where value is to be added – can dictate how some activities are carried out – provides direction and feedback to the project manager
Project sponsor May initiate the project. Normally a senior staff member who adds to the team's authority	– ensures that the project is of relevance to the organisation – helps to set objectives and constraints – may provide resources for the project – is a major contact point for the customer
Project manager Responsible for achieving the project's objectives and leading and motivating the project team	– motivates and develops the project team – produces a detailed plan of action – keeps project stakeholders informed – monitors progress against plan
Team member May have full or part-time involvement in the project, with a specific set of actions to carry out	– takes responsibility for completing specific activities as set out in the plan – may fulfil a specialised role as an expert, or may be needed only for part of the project
Supplier Provider of materials, products or services needed to carry out the project	– can become very involved with, and supportive of, the project – delivers supplies against agreed costs and timescales
Other stakeholder Any of the players in this table, plus anyone else who is interested in, or affected by, the outcome of the project	– can contribute to various stages of the planning process by providing feedback and guidance – may only be involved from time to time, or for a single short period of time

Table 2.1 *Key stakeholders and roles*   Source: *based on Bruce and Langdon* (2000)

As the project manager, you will spend a lot of time working with key players in order to facilitate the project's success.

Selecting your team

One of your first major tasks as project manager is to select your core team – the people with whom you will work most closely. There may be relatively few of these – perhaps half a dozen or less – but the people whom you choose at this stage, and the way that they interact with you and with each other, will play a crucial role in the success of your project.

Putting a team together is no easy task. During the early stages of the project, you may be working with a small core team but even a small team may include people from different work locations, with different expertise and functional responsibilities, different grades and status and different pay. In selecting team members who can work co-operatively together, you will need to choose people who don't just have the right technical skills or experience but have the right interpersonal skills as well.

As suggested by Lockyer and Gordon (1996), these are people who can:

- adopt a problem-solving approach
- freely discuss ideas before they are adopted
- communicate effectively across the team and across different business functions, for example marketing and IT
- sell the team's ideas outside
- get co-operation from people within and outside the team
- make sure that acceptable progress is achieved
- make a sensible assessment of their own and other people's work
- stick together as a team even when things go wrong.

This all assumes that you have a free hand to select your own project team. However, in many organisations the project manager has little or no choice over who will work in the team. In some cases the project manager has to rely on the decisions of other functional managers, for example from accounting, production or design, as to who is available to work on the project. The project manager has then to make the best of the people provided.

Whether you have a free hand or not, getting a diverse group of people to knit together as a team and work towards the common goals of the project is one of the project manager's key roles and key challenges.

Managing your stakeholders

A project's stakeholders are all those people and groups who are interested in, or affected by, the project and its outcomes. They will include customers, suppliers and team members. Your stakeholders are an important group of people – don't underestimate them.

If you have been involved in a project, take a minute to identify all the stakeholders. There are probably quite a few – all with different levels of involvement and interest in what the project was trying to achieve. Clearly the two most important parties are the project sponsor, whose idea it is or who may be putting up the money, and the customer, who will be keen for the project to succeed and deliver the promised benefits. Some stakeholders are active participants; others are passive observers. They will also have different levels of power and influence.

Your stakeholders are potential supporters or opponents of what you're doing or the way you're doing it, with the power to affect other people's opinions for good or ill. You may be able to assess the likely impact of different stakeholders on the project, and identify

Project Management

strategies you can adopt to limit resistance. Both supporting and opposing groups need to be carefully managed. Cultivate your potential supporters as a valuable resource, and where you cannot convert your opponents, try at least to think of strategies to neutralise their influence.

Whether you are building Wembley Stadium or introducing a new customer call-handling system, you will share the joys and tribulations associated with having a diverse set of stakeholders. Ignore them at your peril.

> To identify how your stakeholders are likely to view a project, ask yourself which of them:
> - perceive some benefit to themselves from the success of the project
> - feel threatened by the project or its likely outcome
> - are likely to support it openly
> - are likely to oppose it openly
> - are likely to support it covertly
> - are likely to oppose it covertly.

You can also ask:

> - How can stakeholders influence the success or failure of the project?
> - What level of influence can a stakeholder exert?

Activity 4
Explore the role of stakeholders

Objective

Use this activity to explore the role of stakeholders in a project.

Task

1. Choose a project in which you have been involved or which has affected you.

2. Jot down a list of the project stakeholders – as many as you can think of. For each stakeholder, identify which were:
   - active supporters

2 Project initiation and definition

- ◆ active opponents
- ◆ covert supporters
- ◆ covert opponents.

Add to the list the evidence you have for this.

3 Assess whether their level of influence was high, medium or low.

Project title:

Stakeholder	Supporter or opponent? Active or covert?	Level of influence

Feedback

If you think through the way this particular project proceeded, you may find that the stakeholders exercised more influence (for good or ill) than you had imagined.

You may find it helpful to consider the likely role of the stakeholders for your project right at the start. Who are likely to be active and covert supporters? And who are likely to be active and covert opponents? How much influence do different stakeholders have? This kind of analysis can help you plan how best to manage different stakeholders. Of course, the stakeholders' positions may change as the project progresses, so it is worth keeping informed about their views.

Testing feasibility

There can be many reasons why a good idea fails to make a good project:

- It hasn't been thought through carefully enough: it will take a lot of resources for rather doubtful benefit
- Someone else in your organisation or a competitor has had a similar idea, and is already underway with their project
- There is too much competition for resources from other projects for yours to stand much of a chance
- It's a good idea, but this is the wrong time to turn it into a project
- You do not have the support of key internal stakeholders.

Clearly, there is no point in undertaking any project within an organisation unless it can demonstrate real benefits, and address real needs, such as increasing turnover or productivity, or reducing time to market. Where the project has been requested by a customer who is external to the organisation, it is vital to be confident that you can deliver to expectations. In cases where there is some doubt, it is wise to propose that you carry out a formal feasibility study and share the risks with the customer.

The more urgent or important the need or benefit is seen to be to the organisation, the more likely it is that your project will be agreed. These potential benefits will be the driving forces that work in your favour. At the same time, there will be opposing forces, which work against you. These may include inadequate technology, or out-of-date plant and machinery, not enough people with the right skills, lack of real commitment by management or a key stakeholder group. In order to weigh up the relative strengths of these, you can use a technique called forcefield analysis.

Forcefield analysis

Forcefield analysis is a simple but powerful technique for measuring the strength of both the driving forces and the opposing forces that affect your potential project. By carrying out the analysis, you will be able to see whether the project has a good chance of success, or whether the opposing forces are likely to be too strong.

The analysis is done using a diagram that shows the driving forces on one side and the opposing ones on the other. These are ranked in terms of importance: +5 would be a pressing need while +1 a rather minor benefit. On the minus side, −1 would be a resisting force that you might be able to get around or ignore, and −5 would be a factor which works so strongly against the project that it has a real chance of preventing it from ever reaching its objectives.

Figure 2.1 looks at the driving forces and resisting forces influencing a company's online trading project.

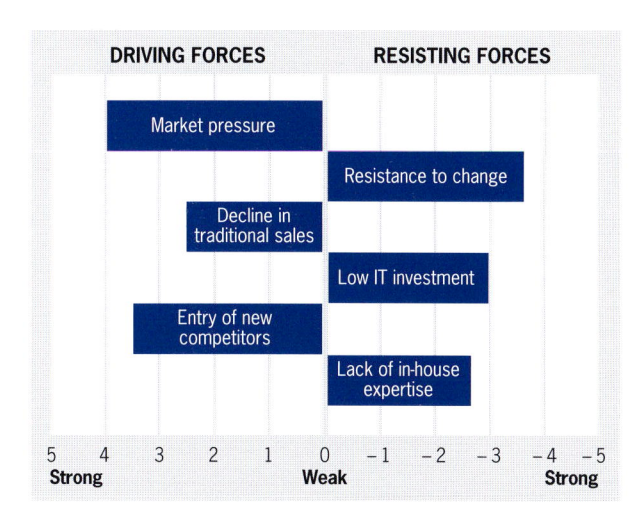

Figure 2.1 *Forcefield analysis on the introduction of online trading*

> As Figure 2.1 shows, the company is subject to strong market pressure to introduce online trading because increasing numbers of customers and suppliers expect this. The threat of new entrants into the marketplace is adding some urgency to the pressure to change. At the same time, the company's traditional sales base is being whittled down. All these forces are driving the company towards introducing online trading facilities.
>
> However, on the debit side, the company is a rather traditional one, and extremely wary of change. It has a history of very cautious investment in IT, and has very limited in-house expertise.
>
> In this example, it seems clear that some radical action is called for if the company is to survive. This will involve trying to effect a shift in organisational culture and making a substantial capital investment in technology, possibly with the short-term assistance of external IT consultants.

You need to be honest and not overoptimistic when identifying both types of force: are you really sure about those benefits? Look hard at the opposing forces: are there any you can neutralise in order to obtain a better balance in favour of your project?

Your proposed project may pass this initial feasibility test – but it is advisable, as the planning progresses, to check this again on a periodic basis with your team members and other stakeholders.

Project Management

Activity 5
Carry out a forcefield analysis

Objective

Use this activity to carry out a forcefield analysis.

Task

1 For the project you chose in Activity 3:

- Identify the driving forces that are working *for* your project
- Identify the forces that are working *against* your project – these are the resisting forces
- Score them on the basis of +1 or –1 for a weak force to +5 or –5 for a strong force.

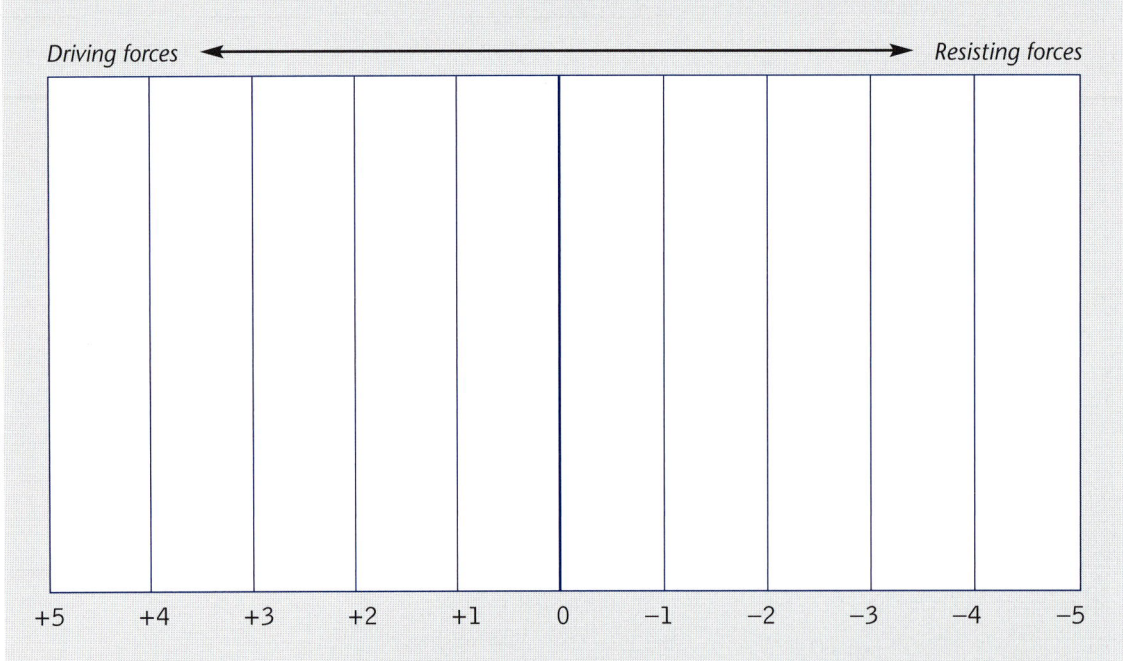

Driving forces ←───────────────────→ *Resisting forces*

| +5 | +4 | +3 | +2 | +1 | 0 | –1 | –2 | –3 | –4 | –5 |

2 Note down your conclusions. How can you minimise the impact of resisting forces?

Conclusions:

2 Project initiation and definition

Agreeing the vision and objectives

A key stage in planning your project is to agree what the project is about. You need to be able to articulate clearly what the project is aiming to achieve and how this adds value to the organisation, customer or stakeholder group.

The vision statement

The vision statement is a clear statement that summarises the project's aims in a way that will be understood by team members and your stakeholders. Of course, the project's aims need to be clearly aligned to business objectives.

Figure 2.2 suggests a process for developing a vision statement. Get your project sponsor and team together and look carefully at what the project is going to achieve, and what will change as a result of it. (If the project has formal Terms of Reference, this aim may already have been expressed in broad terms.) A brainstorming session is a good way of getting some ideas about this. Check out your ideas with your customer. What are their expectations of what this project is, and what it will accomplish?

Where you are involved in managing a project for a customer who is external to the organisation, the process is the same. But here you may have to accept that the customer's vision will be based on their understanding of how the project meets their organisational objectives and constraints.

Unfortunately, there will be times when the customer articulates the vision, and then steps back leaving the project manager to struggle to achieve it. Your customer needs to be managed too – collaborate closely with them at this stage. Your role will be particularly valuable in helping them to think through the vision and all its implications – and if necessary question whether this is really appropriate.

Encourage your team to challenge underlying assumptions, and to question each aspect of the project. The aim of this is to stimulate creativity and new ideas so that the project will achieve some genuine and positive change.

Project Management

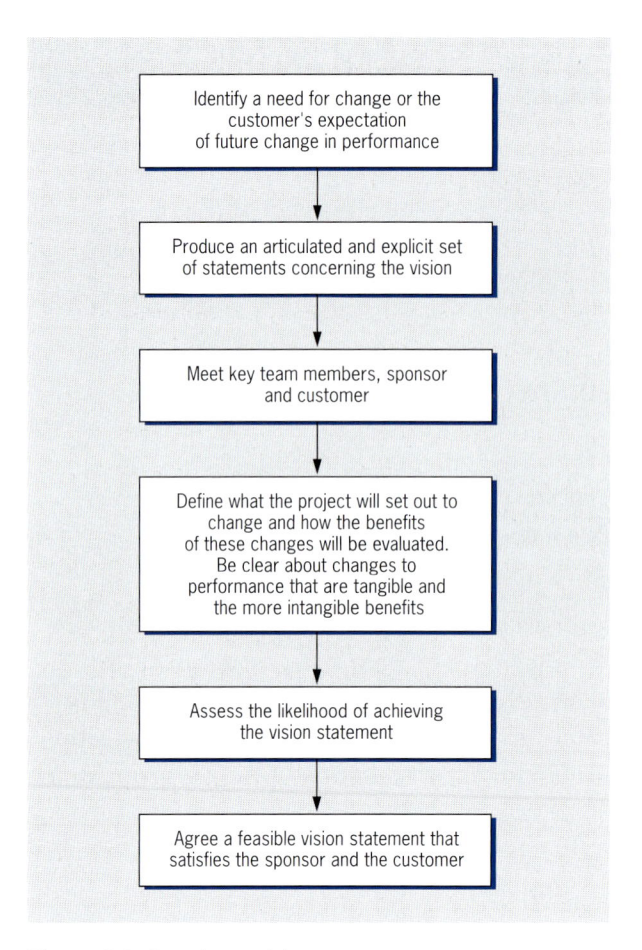

```
┌─────────────────────────────────────┐
│ Identify a need for change or the   │
│ customer's expectation              │
│ of future change in performance     │
└─────────────────────────────────────┘
                  ↓
┌─────────────────────────────────────┐
│ Produce an articulated and explicit │
│ set of statements concerning the    │
│ vision                              │
└─────────────────────────────────────┘
                  ↓
┌─────────────────────────────────────┐
│ Meet key team members, sponsor      │
│ and customer                        │
└─────────────────────────────────────┘
                  ↓
┌─────────────────────────────────────┐
│ Define what the project will set    │
│ out to change and how the benefits  │
│ of these changes will be evaluated. │
│ Be clear about changes to           │
│ performance that are tangible and   │
│ the more intangible benefits        │
└─────────────────────────────────────┘
                  ↓
┌─────────────────────────────────────┐
│ Assess the likelihood of achieving  │
│ the vision statement                │
└─────────────────────────────────────┘
                  ↓
┌─────────────────────────────────────┐
│ Agree a feasible vision statement   │
│ that satisfies the sponsor and the  │
│ customer                            │
└─────────────────────────────────────┘
```

Figure 2.2 *Creating a vision statement*

Source: *Adapted from Bruce and Langdon* (2000)

Setting objectives

> **You got to be careful if you don't know where you're going, because you might not get there.**
>
> **Yogi Berra –
> American baseball star**

Whereas the vision statement sets out a summary of the project and what it will achieve, the objectives describe the detailed means of achieving that vision. They provide direction, a focus on results, and a way of checking back to see whether you are on target. They must have the support of all team members and stakeholders.

The best objectives are SMART, that is:

- Specific
- Measurable
- Achievable
- Results-oriented
- Time-related.

Look at the steps involved in developing SMART objectives. First, put together a list of objectives for discussion with the project team. One, for example, might be to improve response time for handling customer complaints.

In order to test whether this is being achieved, you need to identify an indicator of performance: how do you measure the achievement of your objective? In this case a reduction in the response time is the obvious indicator.

You also need to set targets: not just a reduction in response time, but a reduction from, for example, five working days to 48 hours, with a date by which your objective will be achieved. Remember though, your objectives have to be achievable.

It is likely that you will have a limited number of key objectives – say half a dozen, some of which are clearly more important than others. The team may need to work together to identify objectives and may draw on expertise within or outside the group to identify what needs to be done. Agree with your team which priorities are the most important, the indicators you will use to measure them, and what your targets will be.

Case study: Building an extension to your home
Think about what you would need to consider in preparing a vision statement and objectives for building an extension to your home.

Such a vision statement might embody ambitious changes such as a roof garden or indoor swimming pool, or something more modest like a play area for the children or an additional bedroom. It will also express these outcomes in tangible ways, for example functions of leisure and utility, but also more intangibly, such as pleasure, status, comfort and feelings of well-being. In many projects, particularly those sponsored by an external customer, failure is often attributed to not having delivered on the intangibles. Of course functionality in performance is a key part of the vision and objective setting process, but intangibles are important too.

Objectives might include:
- to increase the floor space by a certain number of square metres
- to allow direct access to the garden
- to provide an enclosed space that is big enough for a single bed and study area
- to provide an environment with an ambience that enhances quality of life.

The last objective is easily overlooked but is probably the key to the success of the whole enterprise.

Identifying key milestones

At this stage you need also to identify the project milestones. These are the achievements that highlight your progress towards successful project completion. Milestones can be expressed in different forms, for example:

- completion of a software prototype
- agreement on the programme for a conference
- registering the hundredth subscriber to a new service
- submitting a design for an architectural competition.

They can also simply represent the completion of a specific phase of a project, which might trigger the production of an interim report.

Checklist
- Do you have a clear project vision statement that everyone is committed to?
- Are your objectives:
  - aligned with wider business objectives?
  - SMART?
  - agreed to by the team and other stakeholders?
- Have you established project milestones?

Activity 6
Evaluate SMART objectives

Objective

Use this activity to assess the importance of SMART objectives.

Task

1 Think of two previous projects you have been involved in, or know about (ideally, one successful and one less so – talk to colleagues if necessary).

2 For each project, establish:
- Were the objectives SMART?
- Were the targets realistic?
- How was progress measured?

2 Project initiation and definition

Project	SMART objectives?	Targets	Progress
1			
2			

3 What was the effect of having (or not having) clear targets and objectives? How did this impact on the success or otherwise of the projects?

Activity 7
Devise SMART objectives

Objective

Use this activity to devise some SMART objectives.

Task

Imagine that you work in a building society which has just launched a new savings product with attractive interest rates. Response has been overwhelming – e-mail and postal enquiries are flooding in. Unfortunately, this far exceeds the anticipated response level, and the company is struggling to get application packs out to prospective applicants in less than two weeks. There is evidence that this delay is not only putting off new customers, but adversely affecting your existing customers, who are interested in this new product but who are used to better standards of service from you.

Project Management

You have been given the task of resolving the problem.

1 What would your SMART objectives be to solve the building society problem?

2 When you have completed these, devise some SMART objectives for your own project.

SMART objectives for the building society problem:

SMART objectives for your own project:

Feedback

The objectives for the building society problem may include:

1 Reduce response time for enquiries from two weeks to seven working days within two weeks of project start.

2 Review mailing arrangements (staffing and procedures) to align with point 1 above.

3 Review application pack stock levels and storage arrangements to align with point 1.

4 Send letter to existing customers within three working days, with an apology for the delay and an explanation.

Scope, constraints and deliverables

You may be clear about the project's vision and broad objectives, but these all have to be achieved within a defining framework.

A failure to define and agree scope is a common reason why projects run into difficulties. Your objectives, indicators and targets may be fine, but unless you have set clear parameters to limit your project, you run the risk of problems later. While you are at this preparation stage, Briner et al. (1997) recommend the five-critical-questions approach that you need to ask of the project:

What is the project's business rationale? Is the project a mainstream activity, related to the organisation's strategic vision, or the whim of an individual or department?

What are the expectations of the different stakeholders? Understanding who the stakeholders are allows the project manager to discuss their expectations, explore alternatives and ensure that the real problem is being addressed.

What will be involved? There needs to be a broad understanding of the activities required to complete the project, so that people can consider its implications.

Do we have the necessary resources? This includes the tangible resources of money, time and materials, and intangible ones like technical skills, commitment and support from key people.

What project results are required? If you understand what the desired impact on the organisation is, then it is easier to work back from there to consider what deliverables will achieve this.

On a practical level, scope needs to be defined in terms of the variables. These are the sorts of issues to think about:

- the units, departments or branches to be covered by the project, for example marketing and sales only
- which groups of staff will be involved – would call handlers and dispatch staff be included?
- location – would activity be restricted to just one region?
- business processes to be involved, for example sales only
- products – would the project be limited to insurance and pensions services, or would it include mortgages?
- limitations on your freedom to make decisions on the use of resources and people
- the freedom that you have to contact outside groups and access information.

The reasons for this should be fairly clear: you need the information to plan activities and to estimate the costs of these. There are other reasons why it is useful to define scope very clearly at the planning stages of a project. If you don't define what's included you don't define what's excluded either, and you might come under pressure to do rather more than you'd intended on the same budget with no easy let-out.

It also avoids disputes with the customer, sponsor and other stakeholders about what it is that you are actually doing. Take great care not to be on the receiving end of phrases like, 'Oh, but I thought you were doing ...' or worse, 'Oh, but your manager told me your project was going to be covering this as well' or, 'This isn't really what we were expecting'.

Time and other constraints

All projects need to achieve a balance between time, cost and quality, and these elements will always have some tension between them. Skimp on cost and the timing may slip and quality suffer; overemphasise quality and costs can escalate.

> **All projects need to achieve a balance between time, cost and quality.**

The time constraints of a project are very rarely within the project manager's control, though the importance of time will vary from project to project. In some cases slippage of a couple of weeks might not matter in other cases a delay of days might be critical.

One of the first things to look at in project planning is the kind of timetable envisaged. What is driving this? For example, consider whether the project is under pressure from internal factors, such as a new MD who wants results quickly. Is it under pressure from external factors, such as anticipated changes in the government budget, the introduction of new legislation or beating a competitor to market? In this latter case, the deadline may be fixed and immovable – you have to meet it, or the project fails.

So – you have your objectives, and you know the time you have to complete your project. You may have been given a budget figure within which to keep. If you have not, this is the time to think about likely costs of the people and other resources you may need. You won't yet be able to do this in any detail – that will happen when you know exactly what you need to do – but you do need to identify the kinds of resources that the project may require. These are some of the questions you may need to ask yourself:

- ♦ If the project team members are doing a lot of travelling around, will they all need laptops? What are the travel costs likely to be?
- ♦ Will the project team need dedicated workspace?

- Are you likely to have all the necessary skills in place, or will team members need training before they can be effective?
- Will you need to employ external consultants?
- Is there any contingency set aside in the budget for managing risks and the unexpected?

Your back-of-envelope calculations may lead you to question the project's viability. But all is not lost. At this point it may be helpful to:

- Revisit and refine your objectives.
- Explore what existing resources you can make use of to cut your time and costs. For example, another department may have carried out a customer survey which, though not completely up to date, is sufficient for your purposes without your needing to commission a fresh one. There may be some technological initiative you can make use of, or there may be expertise hidden away in another department that will save you a consultancy bill.

Don't battle away on your own – consult with your team and stakeholders. Apart from being valuable sources of advice, guidance and information, they need to be clear about the constraints within which the project will need to work. If at the end of your investigations it really does look as if the actual or likely project funding is unrealistic, you have the option of revising the project's vision and objectives or trying to obtain more resources from management.

Deliverables

All projects are required to deliver something as a demonstration that the objectives have been met: a new product, a training course, software or a plan to improve service delivery or customer satisfaction. If the project is lengthy or complex, it will often have interim deliverables: a prototype of some sort, a survey analysis or an interim report. It is common for interim deliverables to be prepared at the end of particular phases of a project, where a specific project target or milestone has been reached.

Interim or final, everyone involved with the project must agree what the deliverables are and when and how they will be achieved. They will provide concrete evidence of a project's progress that will not only reassure management that the project is doing what it set out to do, but also encourage the project team to drive forward with the next stage.

It is important that the customer or client agrees at the start of the project what will be accepted as evidence that the deliverables have been achieved. This can of course backfire when you agree to deliver something which then proves impossible to attain. Getting a balance between prescription and flexibility, and perhaps revisiting resource requirements and deliverables, then negotiating for more resources so that the deliverables can be achieved, is key to success in this area of the project definition.

Now check it out:

- Be clear about what is driving your timetable.

- Take a hard look at your objectives and the ballpark resources required to meet them.

- Note any extraordinary expenditure like equipment, training or consultancy.

- Ask around – what information and other resources can you utilise from elsewhere or recycle, to reduce project costs?

- Look at your objectives again and refine these where necessary. Does the project still have a real chance of success?

> **Case study: Building an extension to your home**
> Think about the constraints and deliverables that will affect a home extension project. Cost will clearly be a major constraining factor. But here are some others that need consideration:
>
> - Can one company carry out all the work, or will some be contracted out?
>
> - How many people will be employed at any one time?
>
> - Will it require specialist architectural services?
>
> - Time is always important: how long will it take to obtain planning consent? Does some of the work need to be done before winter sets in? What happens if the firm with the best estimate is not available until October?
>
> The deliverables should certainly be specified in terms of dimensions, for example excavation, building, etc., materials to be used, standard of finish and installation of services such as water and electricity. However, there are also intangible deliverables that are hard to specify. What most of us would really like to achieve is 100 per cent satisfaction, with no hassle, good humour, lowest cost and on time. The struggle between the builder and the customer is usually over the failure to live up to these expectations. This demonstrates the need for an open and continuous dialogue between both parties around the question of matching expectations to the constraints.

Risk analysis and contingency planning

Projects are risky because they are planned on the basis of assumptions that may look fine now, but may be questionable in the future. For example, a long-running project may be overtaken by events part way through, as the organisation changes its strategic priorities, is subject to a takeover or downsizes in response to falling sales.

> **The afterthought is good, but forethought is better.**
> **Norwegian proverb**

We can reduce the risk to a project that resides in the inherent uncertainties in life and systems but we can only do this when we have made a stab at quantifying these uncertainties and taken actions to minimise their impact.

One very basic assumption, for example, is that you fully understand what it is that the customer wants, and that they will continue to want it. In reality, there is always the risk of producing an outcome that the customer doesn't want or no longer needs.

Sources of risk

All the likely risks in a project need to be identified, assessed and managed, but a good guiding principle is to reduce uncertainty – the more uncertain you are about something, the greater the risk of something going wrong with it. Lockyer and Gordon (1996) have identified a number of sources of risk arising from a project plan:

Timing. All project activities will be tied to a timetable, and made using predictions that will carry some degree of uncertainty. Project activities are estimated internally by the project team or imposed externally, for example you may be dependent on supplier delivery dates. You can be pretty confident about the timing of internal activities as you can use various sources of information, experience of similar projects or knowledge of members of the project team, or about external sources such as professional colleagues or trade publications. For externally timed activities, you need to check the quality and reliability of your suppliers.

Technology. The newer the technology being used on a project, the greater the uncertainty that it will function as planned. The more tried and tested applications you use, the more chance you have that it will behave as predicted.

People. People always introduce an element of uncertainty. Will they be up to the job? Will they get on with each other? You can reduce uncertainty here by making sure that:

- the right skills are in place, and any deficiencies are corrected with training
- you define tasks very clearly to those who have to carry them out

- you have good communications across the project team and with stakeholders.

Finance. Is it going to be enough to complete the project? How financially stable are your suppliers?

Managerial. Maybe your organisation is poor at delegating the necessary authority to its project managers, for example, if they have to work across functions. Or you may have a boss who doesn't trust you to do the job and keeps interfering.

Political. The internal politics of the organisation can have a major impact on the success or otherwise of your project.

> In 1996, one million hectares of forested peatland in Indonesia were cleared to enable rice cultivation in the area. Two and a half years after the scheme began, and after spending US $500 million on it, the project was halted without a single blade of rice being grown.
>
> In 1994, Cunard's £30 million programme for the refurbishment of the QEII badly overran its schedule, resulting in £7.5 million in compensation payments to passengers and major losses to its parent company.

Identifying and responding to risk

Once you have considered all the possible sources of risk, you can look systematically at the different aspects of your project and ask:

- What could possibly go wrong here?
- How likely or unlikely is it that things will go wrong?
- What impact would it have on the project?
- What can you do to avoid or mitigate the risk?

A good idea that will also strengthen your team-building efforts is to brainstorm this within the project team using team members' experience and judgement to identify what the real risks are, and how important they are. Just as your examination of constraints on a project can raise questions about its feasibility, an analysis of risk can also lead you to review project objectives, or decide that the project isn't viable. Remember that project activity and expenditure at every stage is used to reduce the risk of failure and achieve a successful outcome – complex and risk-laden projects are costly by definition.

Calculating the probability of success

A simple method that can be used to provide a quick identification of risk areas in a project is shown in Figure 2.3. The approach relies on your being able to estimate, or at times guess, the probability of success for each of the major stages, and sub-stages, of the project, (note that a probability figure can be between 1 (perfection) and 0 (absolute failure)), and recognising that neither of these is realisable in practice unless you are a magician.

Figure 2.3 is concerned with the project to build an extension on a house. The probabilities of success, for each stage, are multiplied to produce an overall figure of probability of achieving a successful outcome. In this case the figures used show that we are facing a fairly daunting outcome. It tells us that even before starting the project we can anticipate a 10 per cent chance (1 in 10) of achieving satisfaction from all of our combined efforts. Most people would baulk at the thought of going ahead with this project with these kinds of odds, and this confirms our gut feeling that home extension projects fail. In reality, they are built eventually, but a lot of additional money, grief and heartache are expended in getting there.

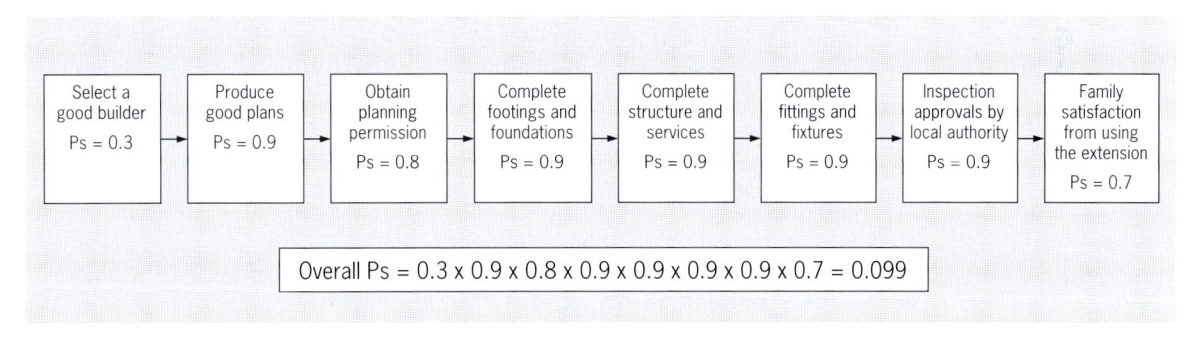

| Select a good builder $Ps = 0.3$ | Produce good plans $Ps = 0.9$ | Obtain planning permission $Ps = 0.8$ | Complete footings and foundations $Ps = 0.9$ | Complete structure and services $Ps = 0.9$ | Complete fittings and fixtures $Ps = 0.9$ | Inspection approvals by local authority $Ps = 0.9$ | Family satisfaction from using the extension $Ps = 0.7$ |

Overall $Ps = 0.3 \times 0.9 \times 0.8 \times 0.9 \times 0.9 \times 0.9 \times 0.9 \times 0.7 = 0.099$

Figure 2.3 *The probability of achieving a successful outcome – home extension project*

Responding to risks

The discerning reader will quickly spot that we are faced with trouble on the project right at the start. We really need to improve the probability of success in selecting the right builder. Perhaps the 0.3 prediction was based on past experience of picking firms from the Yellow Pages with a pin. We also need to focus on improving our chances of getting planning permission at the first attempt, and in conditioning our family's expectations in terms of what joys the new extension will bring.

The trick is to focus our creativity and talent on how to raise the probability of success on these stages, preferably before we begin the project. At least then we can concentrate on the control aspects of the project, rather than being constantly distracted by having to fight those never-ending fires.

If, after considering risks in this way, you're still happy to go ahead with the project, you need to put together a plan for dealing with each of the risks you have identified, and build this into your project plan.

Project Management

Lockyer and Gordon (1996) suggest that there are only a limited number of possible responses to risk:

- modify your project objectives
- use different technologies or methods
- use other ways of managing the project
- increase management strength on the project
- reduce the dependency of one technology or of one task on another
- increase resources
- increase flexibility.

However, there are ways in which you can lower your exposure to risk:

- transfer it to somebody else who is better able to deal with it, for example a subcontractor
- defer it by moving a set of activities to later in the project
- reduce the probability of its occurring
- accept it – and prepare a contingency plan
- avoid it, by changing design or methods.

Activity 8
Conduct a risk analysis

Objective

Use this activity to carry out a risk analysis of your project.

Task

1. List the major stages and sub-stages of your project.
2. For each of these, allocate a probability-of-success (ps) rating. This will vary from 0 (absolute failure) to 1 (total success). Multiply each of the ratings to get a total score.

2 Project initiation and definition

Project stage or sub-stage	Probability-of-success rating

Total score:

3 Put together a plan for dealing with each of the risks you have identified.

Risk	Action to take	When

Project Management

Activity 9
Prepare a project Terms of Reference

Objective
Use this activity to prepare a Terms of Reference document for your project. The Terms of Reference pulls together all the information you have gathered during the project initiation phase.

Task
1. Prepare a Terms of Reference document for your project using the matrix below. (It is understood that at this stage you will not be able to be very specific about resource allocation and activities.)

Project title:	
Project sponsor	
Customer	
Vision statement	
Objectives	
Limitations, exclusions, constraints	
Overall budget	
Resources required	
Deliverables	
Project phases and milestones	
Project risks	
Project staffing: roles and responsibilities	

Source: *Adapted from Brown* (2002)

2 Project initiation and definition

◆ Recap

Identify the key stakeholder groups and consider their likely role in a project

- ◆ Stakeholders are the people and groups who are interested in, or affected by, the project and its outcomes. These include team members, your project sponsor, internal and external customers and suppliers.

- ◆ You need to think about the likely impact of your project on each of your stakeholder groups, to consider whether they might support or oppose you and assess what their degree of influence is likely to be.

Use a forcefield analysis to test the feasibility of a project

- ◆ Forcefield analysis is a technique for testing the feasibility of a project before too much time and money is invested.

- ◆ The relative power of the forces that support and oppose successful completion of the project is compared, and options are generated to alter the balance in favour of supporting forces.

Agree a vision and objectives and key milestones for a project

- ◆ Successful projects result from having an overall vision of how it adds value to the organisation and its customer and from setting SMART objectives that describe the project results or outputs.

- ◆ Key milestones are identifiable achievements that mark progress towards objectives.

Set the scope for a project

- ◆ Setting the scope is another way of defining a project. The scope defines, in precise terms, the range of responsibilities that the project management will (and will not) take on.

- ◆ Engaging closely with customer and stakeholders to develop a shared and unambiguous view of the scope and/or objectives for a project is critical to its success.

Identify and manage potential risks in relation to the project

- ◆ To reduce the risks inherent in a project, you need first to identify their source. Possible sources of risk include timing, technology, people, finance, managerial and political.

- ◆ To help you to identify and respond to risk, ask:
  - What can go wrong here?
  - How likely is this?
  - What impact would it have?
  - What can be done to avoid or mitigate this?

▶▶ More @

Bruce, A. and Langdon, K. (2000) *Project Management*, Dorling Kindersley
This book offers 101 power tips on project management, including how to define your project.

The Project Managemnet Institute (PMI) – www.pmi.org
The *Project Management Body of Knowledge* dedicates chapters to project initiation, scope and risk management. It is available as a download from the Project Management Institute website.

Briner, W., Hastings, C. and Geddes, M. (1997), *Project Leadership*, Gower Publishing
Focusing on the softer sides of project management, this book explores interacting with the project stakeholders.

3 Project planning

Planning is where the vision and objectives are broken down into a series of activities that become the responsibility of specific individuals. The interrelationship between activities, resources and times in most projects, particularly if they are complex, is such that unless they are carefully planned, resources can become seriously overloaded.

This theme explores project planning. The project team, with its blend of people, skills and experience, is an essential platform for project success. You'll start your work in this theme by looking at the mix of roles that a project team needs to achieve results. You'll then move on to look at the essential stages of planning and at the tools and techniques that will help you to get the project ready to launch.

In this theme, you will:

- Review the different kinds of roles that are needed in a balanced project team
- Identify the key activities involved in project planning
- Explore two techniques for developing and documenting project plans
- Consider how to launch the project.

Team roles

To get the initial planning in place, you may have been working with quite a small core team, which will need expansion to get the project started. The kinds of people you approach about their possible involvement in the project will often be dictated by factors outside your control, for example their particular expertise or their availability for the project.

Nevertheless, your views and input are important. How well do you know the person concerned? Are they likely to be enthusiastic about the project, or half-hearted? Will they get on with other team members? Are they bringing the right skills to the project?

> **Do you want a collection of brilliant minds or a brilliant collection of minds?**
> **R Meredith Belbin (www)**

Regardless of the activities they will carry out on the project, every successful team will have members who have one or more distinct team roles to play, whether they are aware of this or not. On his website, Meredith Belbin defines a team role as, 'a tendency to behave, contribute and interrelate with others in a particular way'. Over a period of several years, Belbin and his researchers studied the behaviour of managers from all over the world, who were given psychometric tests and also studied for their behaviour within teams of varying composition. Over time, different clusters of behaviour were identified as underlying the success of the teams, and nine clear team roles emerged:

- action-oriented roles: shaper, implementer and completer finisher
- people-oriented roles: co-ordinator, teamworker and resource investigator
- cerebral roles: plant, monitor evaluator and specialist.

Each of these was seen to offer a unique contribution as team member. Along with their key strengths, Belbin also identified what he called the 'allowable weaknesses' of each role, which the team needs to be aware of so that it can manage them. Table 3.1 describes Belbin's roles in a little more detail.

Team Role Type	Contributions	Allowable weaknesses
Plant	Creative, imaginative, unorthodox. Solves difficult problems	Ignores incidentals. Too preoccupied to communicate effectively
Co-ordinator	Mature, confident, a good chairperson. Clarifies goals, promotes decision-making, delegates well	Can be seen as manipulative. Offloads personal work
Monitor evaluator	Sober, strategic and discerning. Sees all options. Judges accurately	Lacks drive and ability to inspire others
Implementer	Disciplined, reliable, conservative and efficient. Turns ideas into practical actions	Somewhat inflexible. Slow to respond to new possibilities
Completer finisher	Painstaking, conscientious, anxious. Searches out errors and omissions. Delivers on time	Inclined to worry unduly. Reluctant to delegate
Resource investigator	Extrovert, enthusiastic, communicative. Explores opportunities. Develops contacts	Over-optimistic. Loses interest once initial enthusiasm has passed
Shaper	Challenging, dynamic, thrives on pressure. Has the drive and courage to overcome obstacles	Prone to provocation. Ignores people's feelings
Teamworker	Co-operative, mild, perceptive and diplomatic. Listens, builds, averts friction	Indecisive in crunch situations
Specialist	Single-minded, self-starting, dedicated. Provides knowledge and skills in rare supply	Contributes only on a narrow front. Dwells on technicalities

Table 3.1 *Belbin's team role types*   Source: *Belbin* (www)

See www.belbin.com to find out more about Belbin's team roles.

Belbin is not alone in identifying complementary team roles. Another example is given below.

Spencer and Pruss (1992) identified 10 specific team roles, whose function is pretty clear from their titles:

- Confessor
- Librarian
- Coach
- Beaver
- Peacemaker
- Referee
- Challenger
- Explorer
- Pragmatist
- Visionary.

Putting the team together

The point with team roles is that they are all types of behaviour that have been proven to work well in combination within a team environment. This means that to get a really successful team, its members should ideally cover between them the whole range of roles, providing a good mix of the action-oriented, people-oriented and cerebral qualities.

You will always need, for example, someone who is prepared to challenge woolly thinking, someone who will monitor quality, someone who makes sure that team efforts are co-ordinated. You can't do it all yourself. Most people fall naturally into one or two of these categories and may be willing to take on other specific roles if these are missing from the team composition. Of course it helps if they already tend towards this type; there is no point in trying to force a methodical nit-picker to be the team's off-the-wall ideas person.

If you have had very little say in the composition of your team, you may well find that there are gaps, or that you have too many of a particular role type. For example, you may have too many specialists, who try to narrow the team's focus to their own technical preoccupations, or several plants, who generate lots of ideas but never implement anything. Don't ignore this in the hope that the problem will resolve itself once the team gets used to working together – it won't. If it looks as if the make-up of the group might cause problems, consult your project sponsor.

More positively, establishing which roles are temperamentally best suited to you and your team can be a good team-building exercise in itself. If people know themselves a little better, and know what their colleagues' strengths are, there is a better chance that you will all be able to work harmoniously together, and each team member can recognise the value of his or her own and others' contributions.

Project Management

Activity 10
Identify your preferred team role

Objective

Use this activity to identify the kind of role that you are most comfortable with in a team environment.

Background

This activity draws on the team roles explored in the book *Successful Team Building*, by Davis et al. (1992). These team roles are:

- driver
- planner
- enabler
- executive
- controller.

Task

1 Complete the questionnaire below. It consists of five boxes of five statements each. You have 15 points to allocate per box, depending on how strongly you agree with the statements in them. For example, if you agree quite strongly with statement 2: 'I am systematic', you might want to give this five points or more, but you might only want to award two points to statement 3: 'I can usually lay my hands on resources'. If you completely disagree with a statement, you needn't give it any points.

I make a valuable member of any group because ...

1 I am able to see opportunities for group development, and assign responsibilities to group members – without being too domineering

2 I am systematic in my analysis of the group's goals, and can devise plans to help the group achieve them

3 I can usually lay my hands on the resources the group needs to do its job

4 If I'm given a clear objective, I can be relied on to get on with the job

5 I can spot problems as they arise and show the group how to get back on track

Total   15

3 Project planning

I would usually be invited to join a group because …

6. I'm good at checking the methods the group uses, and make sure that there are procedures covering all major activities
7. I can be relied on to be strong and give direction to other team members
8. I can estimate rapidly what resources the team needs – and what they will cost
9. I can spot good ideas quickly – and get the rest of the group enthused about them
10. I'm good at giving the day-to-day guidance that results in smooth workflow and good working practices

Total   15

I feel most satisfied when …

11. promoting good teamwork and helping the team to work better together
12. carefully analysing situations, weighing the evidence and drawing conclusions
13. engaged in work that stretches my creativity and allows full flight to my imagination
14. using tried and tested methods to produce new output
15. working out a deal face-to-face with people who may have something new to offer

Total   15

When my team is to work on a specific project …

16. my ability to get the right resources to the right place at the right time eliminates delays
17. my ability to follow instructions and get through the work assigned to me gives the group a fair chance of producing what is needed
18. my vigilance helps the team to identify and hopefully overcome barriers to high achievement
19. my ability to keep the team focused on its goals makes sure it delivers what is expected
20. my care in analysing the goals prevents us missing out activities and procedures

Total   15

If I were to congratulate myself at the end of a project it would most likely be because …

21. my ability to budget for the project had ensured efficient use of resources
22. my ability to whip up enthusiasm for the project meant that the team cared about the result
23. my ability to structure tasks and organise the work flow kept the group highly productive
24. my ability to identify areas of greatest risk showed the team the best opportunities for improvements
25. my capacity for valid judgement gave the team someone to rely on to make major decisions and give clear direction

Total   15

My major contribution to teamwork is …

26 having good ideas and coming up with novel ways of solving the group's problems

27 working out the best way of organising the work to minimise wasted effort

28 getting people to agree on actions that leave everyone satisfied

29 quickly sensing when people are tense or stressed, and helping them talk through their problem

30 feeding back to the group information about the extent to which it is achieving, or has achieved, its goals

	Total	15

If asked which part of the work gives me most satisfaction, I would say that I most enjoy …

31 observing the group, keeping them on course and performing well

32 deciding how the group should develop and making sure that it does

33 analysing goals, assessing risks and choosing the best course of action

34 making sure that the group has the best materials and equipment with which to produce its output

35 doing something that is neither too difficult, nor too easy, but which gives me a sense of achievement

	Total	15

I would describe myself as someone who most of the time …

36 enjoys working with the group to find practical solutions to operational problems

37 enjoys work that enables me to satisfy my inquiring, investigative nature

38 likes to exert strong influence on the group's decisions

39 enjoys work that demands a systematic and thorough approach

40 enjoys selling ideas, services or products

	Total	15

I'm welcome in group problem solving sessions because of my ability to …

41 give and take in my dealings with other team members, though I will try to persuade them to my point of view

42 maintain a working environment in which the group can freely and openly discuss their views

43 question the effectiveness and efficiency of each element of the team's activity to identify the real problems and their causes

44 bring a degree of ingenuity and creativity to group problem solving

45 fix the agenda and timetable for the activity.

	Total	15

Scoring

Enter the score you gave for each phrase into the box of the question number below:

1	7	13	2	8
19	25	26	20	21
32	38	44	33	39
Characteristic A	Characteristic B	Characteristic C	Characteristic D	Characteristic E
14	3	9	15	4
27	16	22	28	17
45	34	40	41	35
Characteristic F	Characteristic G	Characteristic H	Characteristic I	Characteristic J
10	11	5	6	12
23	29	18	24	30
36	42	31	37	43
Characteristic K	Characteristic L	Characteristic M	Characteristic N	Characteristic O

Your scores should show as three entries in each block column. Add the totals of each column, and write these in the box titled A, B, etc. This gives you your preference score for each of the characteristics, which go together to make up one role.

Now transfer each characteristic total to the role boxes below: totals A, B and C under Driver, totals D, E and F under Planner and so on. (N.B. no characteristic should total more than 15 points.) Add the totals for the characteristics together to get your role scores.

When you have worked out all the role totals, check that they add up to 135.

The highest score is your primary preferred role, the next highest your secondary role. Do you have a third role that scores more than 30? It is more likely that you only show the occasional high characteristic score in other roles.

Example

A: Developer	11	A: Developer	D: Strategist
B: Director	9	B: Director	E: Estimator
C: Innovator	12	C: Innovator	F: Scheduler
DRIVER	**32**	**DRIVER**	**PLANNER**
G: Resource manager		J: Producer	M: Monitor
H: Promoter		K: Co-ordinator	N: Auditor
I: Negotiator		L: Maintainer	O: Evaluator
ENABLER		EXECUTIVE	CONTROLLER

Source: *Davies et al.* (1992)

This is what they all mean:

Driver

A Driver is an intuitive decision maker, who uses instinct rather than analysis. Forward-looking, a risk taker and someone who loves change and life in the fast lane, the Driver is more interested in the big picture than the detail, and prefers to tell than sell. Drivers are enthusiastic organisers and team developers.

Within the Driver group, the Developer will identify directions for the team, clarify opportunities, ensure that the team grows along lines that suit it best, and builds the team's power and influence. The Director is dissatisfied with the way things are, and sees improvement as a challenge. Directors get things done – usually by others. They originate action, and will demand, instruct or coerce to get what they want done. The Innovator is the cornerstone of the team's creative effort. Imaginative and ingenious, the Innovator acts as the catalyst for the team, setting the team's sights on new opportunities and introducing new methods to improve the probability of the team's success.

Planner

The Planner is a logical thinker, who will analyse in depth, diagnose in detail and judge with confidence. They will take the Driver's 'required' future and interpret it in a way that the team can understand and use. Planners are organised and orderly, comfortable with regular procedures and conservative in their approach to change. They are forward-looking, and good at setting targets. They set high standards for themselves and others.

Within the Planner group, the Strategist can take a loosely defined aim and develop it into a detailed strategic statement. They can visualise the organisation needed to achieve the aim, how to build it and the effect it will have on the people involved. They can link what has gone before with the future and see what might go wrong. The Estimator assesses how much work the team is capable of doing, and by interpreting the strategy, judges what capacity is likely to be required.

They will analyse the strategic goals in order to determine what resources the team will need. The Scheduler analyses the tasks to be performed by the team, and works out which tasks are best suited to each role, which activities to combine, and which must be performed in sequence or in parallel. They determine what resources are needed and when and where they are required.

Enabler

Enablers rely on their personal values to direct their decisions. They are natural sales people, and work to convert people to their point of view. Outgoing and persuasive, they are enthusiastic for anything new. They are not always well organised, but they will take on a plan and make sure that the team gets the resources it needs to follow it through.

Within the Enabler group, the Resource Manager understands the nature of the resources needed by the team and how they should be used and controlled. They are best at identifying the resources the team will need for its future activities, noting any problems and updating the Planner. The Resource Manager is the person who will consider the personal development of team members and identify appropriate training. The Promoter will publicise the team's successes, selling the team to everyone outside, and selling the plans and the future to team members. The Promoter will also highlight goals and strategies, raise team enthusiasm and work to overcome resistance to change. The Negotiator gives the team a realistic view of the outside world. They have a clear picture of the people with whom the team must negotiate, people who can either help or block progress. The Negotiator will identify what people expect from the team and how satisfied they are, and will make proposals for improvements to the team output and bargain for team resources.

Executive

If you are an Executive, you will base decisions on observation and how you feel about what you see. They are realists – there is a job that needs doing, so they do it. They are capable of turning instruction into action, systematically, patiently and completely. They live in the present and are not too worried about what the future might bring. The Executive will make great efforts to ensure that the team works in harmony to get things done.

Within the Executive group, the Producer puts plans and instructions into action. These are the goal setters and goal achievers, but they are also realists – they don't try to achieve the impossible. Producers need a system or procedures to follow (creating their own if necessary), and will participate in job design and organising workflow. The Co-ordinator is best at balancing the varied and conflicting demands placed on the team by different parts of the organisation, and makes sure that each team member has their fair share of day-to-day work and individual tasks. They will develop and regulate the team's standards of behaviour, and will organise individuals into a working team. The Maintainer is the person who holds the team together.

Natural counsellors, they can spot conflict early on, and help those involved to resolve the issues. They can help all team members to set realistic goals and workable strategies, and give continual support to the group.

Controller

The Controller is an analytical thinker, who will base their decisions on an analysis of what happened in the past. Controllers enjoy developing a detailed understanding of the way the team works, the systems it uses, the progress it is making and the results it has achieved. They use their experience and knowledge to give advice and guidance on target setting and the solution of problems, and can assess in detail the costs incurred by the team's operations and the benefits achieved by it.

In the Controller group, the Auditor will analyse the team's activities in detail. They will check that resources are of adequate quality to match the activity, and will check for errors and their cause. The Monitor will produce the team's formal records. They will observe the team in operation, in the work it does and as a group working together, to ensure that the team is following procedures, and will provide feedback on this to the Planner. Monitors are the progress chasers. The Evaluator is the team's judge or quality manager, able to assess in detail the costs and benefits of the team's operation. The Evaluator will report whether the team has provided what was asked for, when needed, to the right standard, and at cost within budget. They will provide feedback to show if the team's choices were wise and its efforts really successful.

Feedback

> Were you surprised by your results from completing the questionnaire? Listen and watch carefully in your next team meeting! You may want to use this activity to identify the preferred roles of your own team members. Bear in mind that even though you may prefer to adopt one particular team role, you may need to take on other roles in order to enable the team to work effectively.

3 Project planning

Work breakdown structure and task definition

The Work Breakdown Structure (WBS) is the document that translates your objectives into a list of specific and concrete activities or tasks – the project menu, if you like. Its purpose is to:

- ensure that every aspect of the project has been covered adequately and that there are no gaps
- enable detailed resource planning
- allocate responsibilities for tasks to specific individuals or groups.

The process can start within the project team with a brainstorm. Draw on their expertise – they know the work they do and what is involved better than anyone else.

Make a list of every possible activity that you can think of that will be needed to carry out the project. Your project will of course be unique, but there may have been a similar one, perhaps involving one of your team, whose WBS you can use for guidance.

The next stage is to group the activities together logically into a series of phases or stages, which will broadly follow the timetable of the project.

One possible way of doing this is set out in Figure 3.1. This demonstrates the way that project activities are grouped together and can be broken down into different levels.

> **The secret of getting ahead is getting started. The secret of getting started is breaking your complex, overwhelming tasks into small manageable tasks – then starting on the first one.**
>
> **Mark Twain (1835–1910)**

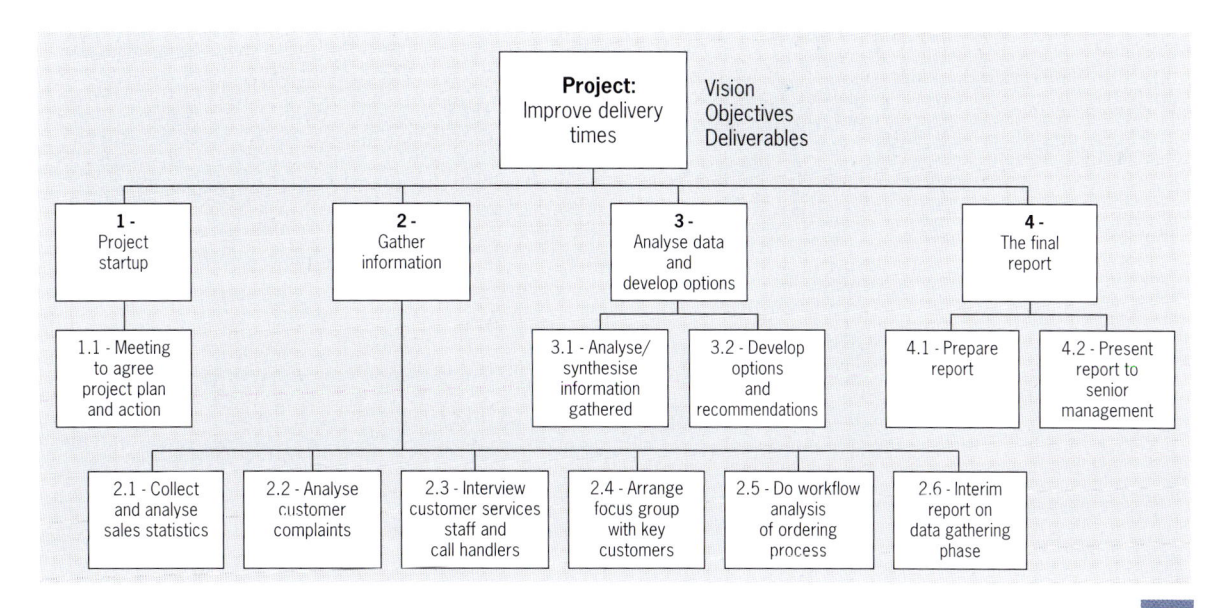

Figure 3.1 *Part of a Work Breakdown Structure*

Some activities tend to group very easily together; others are more difficult to fit into a framework. For some you will need to establish whether they are really a separate task, or part of something else. Are they absolutely necessary to the project? Keep checking back against the project objectives to make sure.

Make sure that the project milestones are incorporated into your project structure. In Figure 3.1, task 2.6 signifies the end of the data-gathering phase.

When you have a reasonable draft WBS, ask your team to check for gaps and consult some of your stakeholders. They may see things that you have missed, or have useful guidance to offer on the way activities have been grouped.

You will end up with activities at two or more levels: Figure 3.1 only has two levels, but can be broken down to a further layer of detail.

For example, task 3.1 – (Analyse/synthesise information gathered) could be divided into: task 3.1.1 (Customer views) and task 3.1.2 (Staff views), and subdivided further if, for example, you wanted customer views by market segment, or to analyse the information gathered from different groups of staff as separate tasks.

> **Some questions to ask yourself:**
> - If we complete all the activities listed, will we meet all the project's objectives?
> - Will the activities ensure we hit our targets?
> - Does our activity list reflect the priorities we originally set for each objective?
> - Have we written down the activities in sufficient detail?
> - Are all the activities listed really necessary?

Source: *Bruce and Langdon* (2000)

Statement of work (SOW)

Once you have agreed the tasks you will perform, and how these will be grouped, you can give the responsibility for doing them to the task owners. The task owner can be a single individual, with responsibility for carrying out one task or a whole group of tasks. Another option you might like to consider is to give each member of the core team responsibility for different aspects of the project, and for managing their own sub-teams. Both of these will require you, as the project manager, to understand fully the skills, competencies and technical expertise needed by the task, and the degree to which the task owner can provide these.

The task owner must take responsibility for all aspects of the task. For example, in Figure 3.1, task 2.4 (Arrange focus group with key customers), will include:

- identifying which customers to approach
- getting agreement for their involvement
- arranging a date for the meeting
- booking accommodation and refreshments
- arranging for any necessary equipment, for example a video camera and/or someone to take detailed notes
- writing up a report on the session afterwards.

You will see that this task links up with tasks 2.1 (Collect and analyse sales statistics), 2.2 (Analyse customer complaints) and 2.3 (Interviews with customer services staff and call handlers.) Look at linkages like these for guidance in scheduling the tasks – for example, do you want to talk to the customers before you talk to the staff, or vice versa?

Each task will have a SOW describing the activities, who is to carry them out, when, and with what resources. It will also include any reporting requirement. Each SOW must be agreed between the project manager and the task owner.

Activity 11
Prepare a Work Breakdown Structure

Objective

Use this activity to prepare a Work Breakdown Structure (WBS) for your project.

Task

As a practice run, construct a Work Breakdown Structure for a project to build an extension onto your house.

1. Begin by defining what the phases will be. Where will you start? How many different stages of the project do you envisage?
2. Then break down each stage into its constituent tasks.

Project Management

Stage 1:

Task 1.1

Task 1.2

Task 1.3

Stage 2:

Task 2.1

Task 2.2

Task 2.3

Stage 3:

Task 3.1

Task 3.2

Task 3.3

3 Repeat the process for the stages of your own project. Test these out with the people involved.

Stage 1:

Task 1.1

Task 1.2

Task 1.3

Stage 2:

Task 2.1

Task 2.2

Task 2.3

Stage 3:

Task 3.1

Task 3.2

Task 3.3

3 Project planning

Feedback

Your first group of activities will involve research and information gathering. This includes checking Yellow Pages for builders and architects, perhaps looking through magazines to get some design ideas, and visiting specialist building suppliers to see what kinds of brick, windows and flooring might be available. The next phase will probably be project planning, that is arranging for planning permission, getting quotations from a range of builders, selecting an architect, etc. You will probably end up with around 10 activities in all.

Resource plan and commitment matrix

It is the task owner's job to estimate the resources required to carry it out. However, as the project manager, you will need to set this into the wider picture, and calculate how feasible the resource requirement is, before agreeing it with the task owner, or sending them off to think again. Bruce and Langdon (2000) have provided a useful summary of the stages involved in considering key resources. See Figure 3.2.

PEOPLE

| How many people do you need? | → | Assess who will take on each activity |

| What type of skills do they require? | → | Identify levels of expertise required |

OTHER RESOURCES

| What facilities, materials and supplies are needed? | → | Look at what each activity requires |

| What information and technology is needed? | → | Examine using existing systems |

MONEY

| What is the total cost of the project? | → | Consider the cost of all the resources |

| Are sufficient funds available? | → | Check the budget that was agreed |

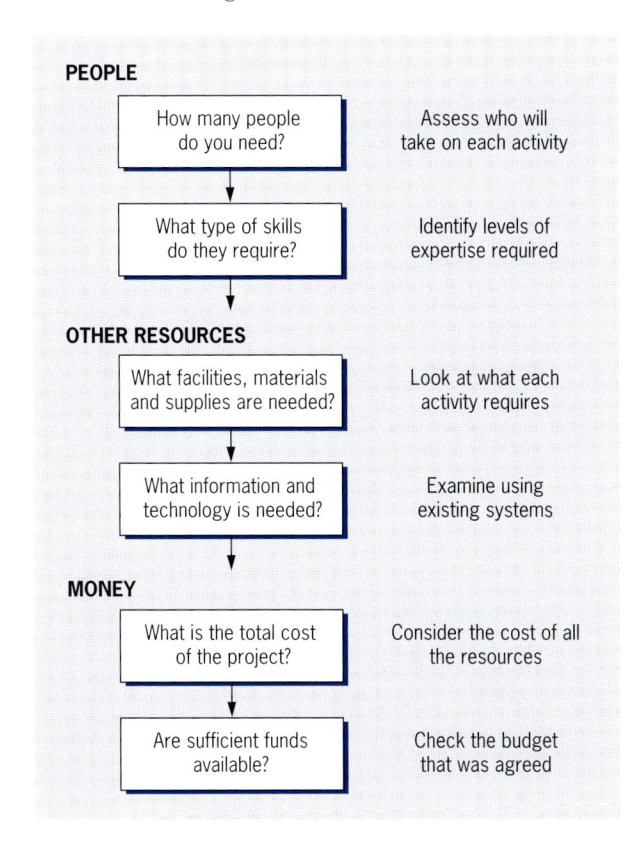

Figure 3.2 *Considering key resources*

Brown (2002) has set down some basic principles for estimating:

- Estimates should be expressed in terms of the actual days worked to complete the task – not elapsed time, which is the period over which the activity will happen
- Don't include contingency time here – add this on globally at the end
- Keep your estimates honest
- Get individual commitment
- Allow for staff skills and experience levels
- Document the procedure used and any assumptions made
- Revisit the process throughout the project to make sure the assumptions still hold
- Make sure every aspect is reasonable.

People

You may be clear by this stage who you want to involve in terms of the project team, but you will need to think carefully about how they are used. Are there people who are effectively full time on the project, who will just join it for a short time, or who will be used intermittently as a source of expert advice? If a task requires a short amount of time each day over a long period, what is the person doing the rest of the time? If they are seconded to your project and have no other work to do, this could prove to be extremely expensive.

Don't forget to calculate your own time – project management is a major activity.

This is the time to double check that your team has all the necessary skills in place, and to identify training if necessary.

Other resources

These can come in many different forms. For example, you may need a substantial travel budget, to hire facilities for a focus group, to pay for training, to buy a dedicated piece of equipment for the project, to hire outside consultants or to translate the final report for dissemination to your offices in the Far East.

Calculating these is most easily done on an activity-by-activity basis. For equipment, it is well worth checking to see whether what you need already exists within the organisation and can be made available to the project.

Don't overlook the use of internal organisational knowledge as a resource – if you have identified a skills gap, it might be possible to fill it by arranging informal training in-house, rather than an expensive external course. Don't forget that resources also cover any office accommodation that the team may require, and meeting-room space.

If you need to use outside contractors or consultants for any part of the project, you will need to prepare clear Terms of Reference, and get quotations from a range of companies. If your organisation has a formal tendering procedure, you will need to follow it – check how long the process is likely to take, and whether it will impact adversely on your project.

Money

You should now be in a position to add up all your project costs and compare this to your overall budget figure. Have you got sufficient funding for your project to succeed? If you need to negotiate for more, this may be your last chance.

In costing out your project, you may have to follow existing procedures within the organisation. You have a choice of two methods: absolute costing or marginal costing. In absolute costing, the exact cost of the resource is charged to the project. For example, if you buy a dedicated piece of equipment for the use of the project, the whole amount is charged to the project, though if you use existing equipment, perhaps borrowed from another department, only a percentage is charged. In marginal costing, a cost is only incurred if the project uses a resource that would not otherwise be used by somebody else. If your borrowed laptop or flipchart has been languishing in a cupboard for months, the cost of your using it is nil, so it does not become a project cost.

Whatever the costing method, you need to take a very hard look at your expenditure and ask yourself:

- Is there a cheaper way of doing this?
- How essential is it as an activity?
- Is the right person doing it?
- Have all the additional resources that we need been identified?

The commitment matrix

The plan of resources required may need a number of passes and compromises before you can produce a final version that all project stakeholders can agree to. These resources can all be documented in the commitment matrix (see Table 3.2) an at-a-glance view of tasks, resources and costs.

Activity	People			Resources			Cost
	Who is responsible?	Who is involved?	Training needs	Facilities	Equipment	Materials	
2.1	AJB (2 days)	RHC (5 days)	Interview techniques (1 day)	Meeting room Syndicate rooms (2 days)	OHP (1 day) Chart (1 day) Computer (1 day)	Market research report	£23,500

Table 3.2 *Commitment matrix*   Source: *Bruce and Langdon* (2000)

Project network techniques

Your resource plan and commitment matrix will give you the essential first stages of constructing a network diagram: a list of activities and their duration. You also need to determine in which order the activities will be carried out.

Activities, times and dependencies

The list of tasks that make up your project will include the number of person-days required to carry them out, but there are other things you need to know:

- Elapsed time. What is the start and end date for the activity (i.e. how much time will have elapsed between start and finish)? A questionnaire survey may take only four days in realtime, but four weeks in elapsed time, from questionnaire design to return of completed forms. Be realistic about elapsed time, and look at your best and worst case scenarios. Make sure that you and the task owner agree about how long this task will take.

- What is the activity dependent on? Is there another activity that needs to be completed before this one starts?

- What is dependent on this activity? What other activities can't start until this one is finished? If you want your interviews to pick up on points made by questionnaire, this will determine the sequence of these activities.

- What activities can be done simultaneously with this one? Some activities are totally independent from others and can be done while other work is progressing.

A network diagram is a graphic representation of activities over time and the dependency relationship between them.

By establishing what the dependency relationship is between the different tasks, we can build up a dependency network. The main purpose of this is to determine the critical path through the project timetable. The critical path is the shortest possible time needed to complete the project.

These days, automated planning tools will do much of the hard work for you. If you are just about to embark on a project, you will need to find out what project management software your organisation uses, and arrange appropriate training. There are many different kinds of project management software, geared to projects of different levels of complexity.

A lot of information on software is available on the Internet – try sites such as www.4pm.com for a buyer's guide to selecting project management software, which includes a list of vendors. Another useful source of information is the Project Management Centre's Directory of Project Management Software, at www.infogoal.com.

However, even if the software is doing a lot of the work, you will still find it useful to understand the principles of network diagrams.

Project network techniques

There are two broad types of project network technique: Activity on Arrow (AoA) and Activity on Node (AoN). Both are detailed below, because your organisation may favour using one or the other. But for simplicity and ease of use, most projects adopt the AoA approach. We suggest you focus on one approach – that chosen by your organisation.

Activity on Arrow (AoA)

The AoA system, sometimes referred to as critical path analysis or PERT, Program Evaluation and Review Technique, consists of a network made up of two basic elements:

1 An activity – that is, a necessary element of work in a project.

   It can be a 'real' activity or a 'non-work' activity. A real activity uses real resources, for example interview sales staff. A non-work activity does not involve a physical task, but is still an essential part of the project, for example awaiting the return of questionnaires.

   There are also dummy activities, which are occasionally inserted into a network diagram to give its logic greater clarity (we will look at these in a moment). AoA activities are expressed in the form of an arrow in the network diagram, see Figure 3.3.

Figure 3.3 *Using AoA diagrams (1)*

Note that the arrow-head is at the completion of the activity.

2   An event or node, which is the start or finish of an activity or group of activities. These nodes are usually shown as circles containing a convenient label, like a number – Figure 3.4.

Figure 3.4 *Using AoA diagrams (2)*

> Some points to note:
> - The flow of activities always goes from left to right.
> - The node number at the head of the arrow is always higher that the node number at the tail of the arrow. This means that activities can be referred to by their tail and head numbers, such as activity five-six, which means the activity that starts at five and finishes at six.
> - Only dependent activities connect nodes.
> - It is not necessary for all numbers to be in strict sequence – in fact, it can be useful to leave gaps in the numbering so that additional nodes can be added later without having to amend the whole network diagram.

Figure 3.5 shows a single activity and Figure 3.6 shows that Activity B is dependent on Activity A.

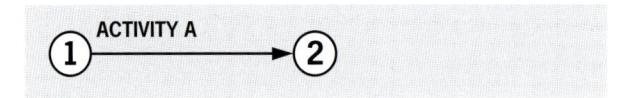

Figure 3.5 *Using AoA diagrams (3)*

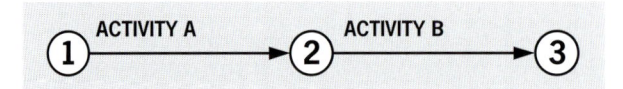

Figure 3.6 *Using AoA diagrams (4)*

Figure 3.7 illustrates a simple everyday example. In Figure 3.7 you can see that the cake-cutting and tea-making activities can proceed in parallel, but the washing-up is dependent upon finishing both of them.

3 Project planning

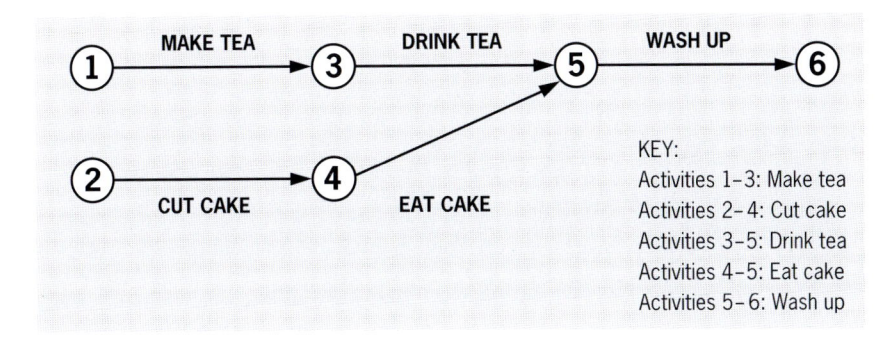

Figure 3.7 *Tea time*

Dummies

In the example in Figure 3.7, drink tea and eat cake have different tail nodes but the same head node. It sometimes happens that two or more parallel activities can have the same head and tail nodes. In this case, it is sometimes clearer to put in a dummy activity to avoid two different activities having the same head and tail numbers.

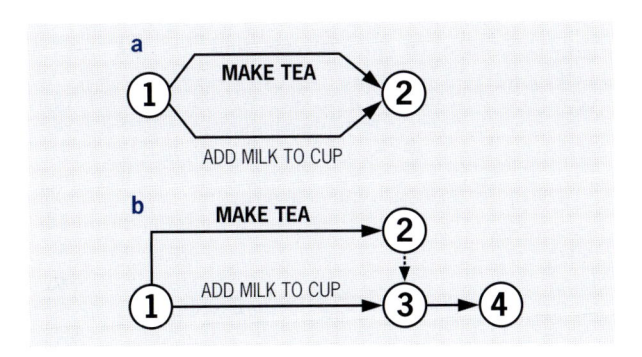

Figure 3.8 *Using dummy activities*

Figure 3.8 (a) shows two activities with the same head and tail number. In order to get round this problem, dummy activity 2-3 has been inserted in example (b).

Activity arrows have the time needed to complete the task recorded under the arrow in consistent time units – normally hours, days or weeks. The time units used in the tea example in Figure 3.9 are minutes. Note that dummy activities have zero time.

Figure 3.9 *Showing time*

Now let's see how this technique might work for the project to improve delivery times, see Figure 3.10.

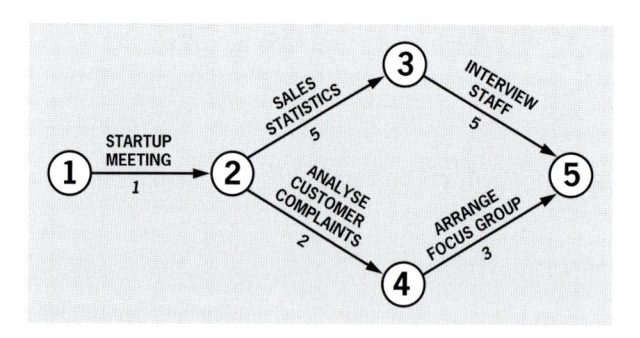

Figure 3.10 *AoA network for project to improve delivery times*

The total project time (TPT) is the shortest time in which the entire project can be completed. This is also known as the critical path. In Figure 3.10 you can see this critical path will take 11 days (1 + 5 + 5). Identifying the critical path, and if necessary adjusting project times or the project logic, is an essential part of evolving the best plan for carrying out the project activities, and making sure that you are making the most intelligent use of the time and resources available.

With a simple set of activities that are drawn to scale on a left-to-right time grid it is possible to calculate the resource usage over time. Software packages also provide data that allows you to adjust activity start times so that you have the resources you need to complete the activities in the allocated time frame.

Activity on Node (AoN)

An Activity on Node (AoN) network also has two basic elements:

1. An activity: like an AoA activity, this can be an actual activity or a 'waiting for something to happen' type activity. This activity is represented by a node, which is usually depicted as a rectangle. Take care not to confuse these nodes with AoA nodes.

Figure 3.11 *Using AoN diagrams (1)*

2. A dependency arrow that shows the interrelationship between various activities. If Activity B depends upon Activity A, it must follow it as shown in Figure 3.12.

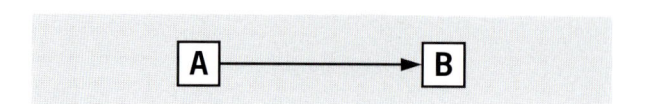

Figure 3.12 *Using AoN diagrams (2)*

3 Project planning

Figure 3.13 shows a situation where C is dependent upon A, and D depends on A and B:

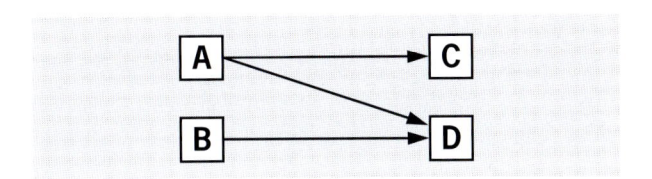

Figure 3.13 *Using AoN diagrams (3)*

Note that your arrows can't cross each other and that AoN diagrams have no dummy activities. In AoN, the dependency-time – the time that must elapse between starting one activity and starting its dependent or following activity – is put under the dependency arrow. The activity's duration-time is put into the node box – Figure 3.14.

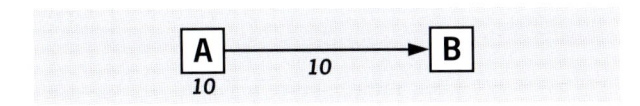

Figure 3.14 *Using AoN diagrams (4)*

In Figure 3.14, B can't start until A is finished. Therefore, the time taken to complete A is exactly the same as the dependency time. However, if B can start partway through Activity A – say three days after A has started – the dependency-time will reflect this. See Figure 3.15.

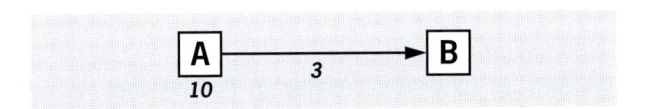

Figure 3.15 *Using AoN diagrams (5)*

As in AoA networks, any activities that are not linked by a dependency relationship can take place simultaneously. See Figure 3.16.

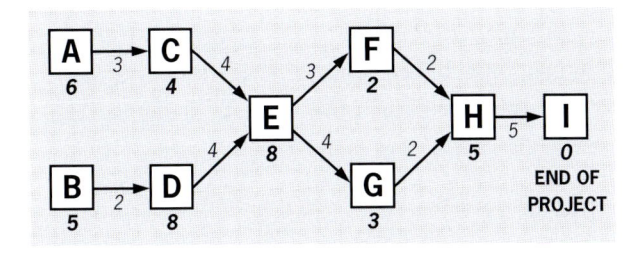

Figure 3.16 *AoN network*

In the diagram in Figure 3.16:

- E is dependent upon C and D. It can't start before C is finished but can begin halfway through D.
- F and G depend upon E, but can both start before E finishes.

Project Management

- I is the end of the project, and is added for neatness.

Finally Figure 3.17 is an AoN diagram showing the same activities on the project to improve delivery times.

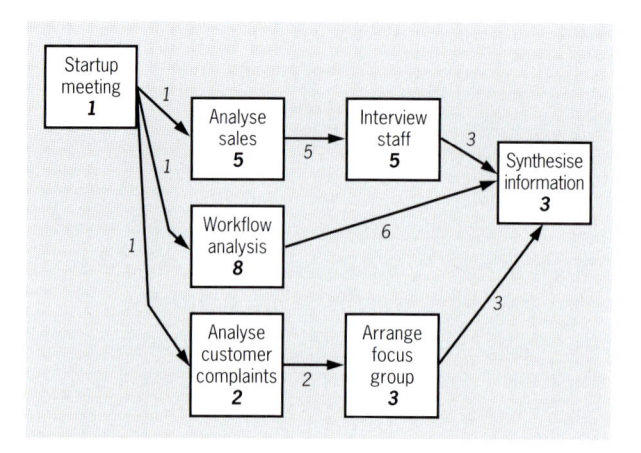

Figure 3.17 *AoN network for project to improve delivery times*

Network diagrams are very powerful diagnostic tools, but can be complex as working documents. Senior managers will not be prepared to spend time deciphering the logic and sophistication of the planning documentation, and will be looking for an at-a-glance view of the project. For this you can use Gantt charts.

Activity 12
Construct an Activity on Arrow diagram

Objective

Use this activity to construct an Activity on Arrow (AoA) diagram.

Task

Choose a project in which you are involved or use the one you have been planning through this book. Identify the tasks that will make up the first phases of your project and construct an Activity on Arrow diagram.

3 Project planning

Activity on Arrow diagram

Feedback

You will have seen that network diagrams can be quite complex, even when the activities they cover are straightforward. However, they do provide a clear and detailed breakdown of activities.

You may find it helpful, if you are new to the technique, to discuss it with a colleague who has some experience of network diagrams.

Project software tools can make network diagrams easier to prepare, but it is useful to understand the principles.

Project Management

Gantt charts

Gantt charts give an overview of a project. The Gantt chart is likely to be the document that summarises all the plans for the project. It provides an at-a-glance view and so is especially useful for presenting to stakeholders and your project sponsor – when you're ready for the go-ahead.

What is a Gantt chart?

A Gantt chart, in its simplest form, consists of two elements: task and time. Tasks can be specified as individual pieces of work, or aggregated upwards into blocks of activities or whole stages. Time will normally be broken down into periods of weeks or months, depending on the length of the project. Time periods are normally numbered, as in the example in Figure 3.18, or dated, for example w/c 14 May. The length of elapsed time allocated to each activity is then blocked out on the timetable.

PROJECT: IMPROVE DELIVERY TIMES

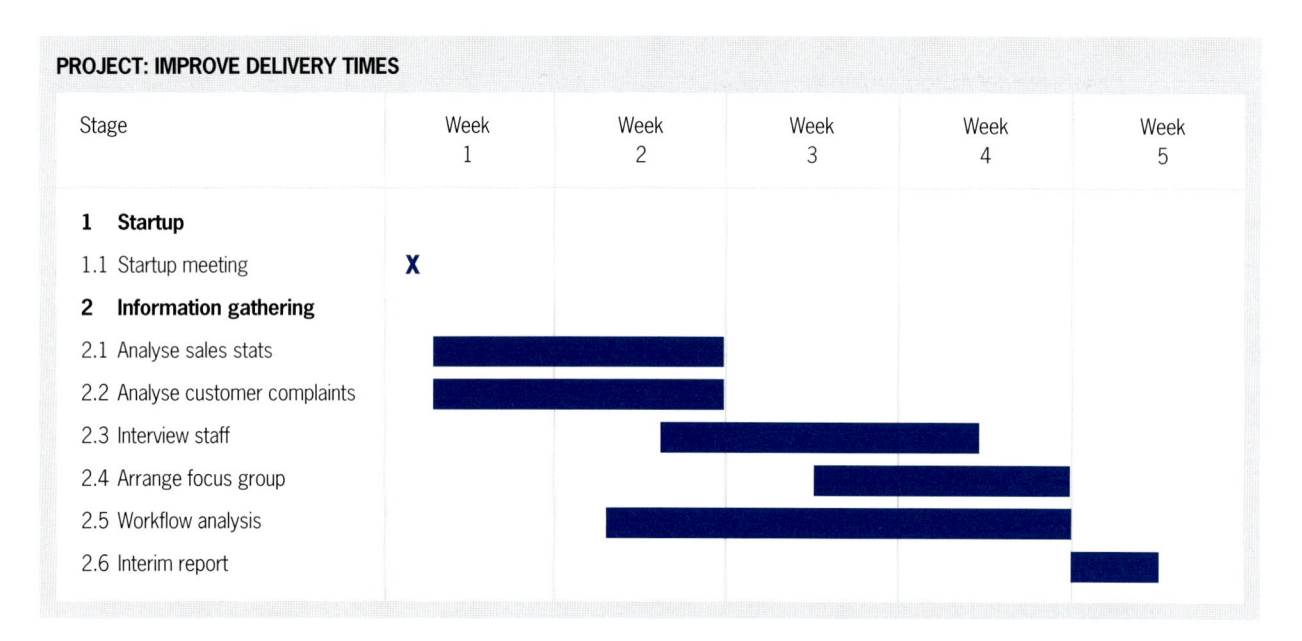

Stage	Week 1	Week 2	Week 3	Week 4	Week 5
1 Startup					
1.1 Startup meeting	X				
2 Information gathering					
2.1 Analyse sales stats	▬▬▬	▬▬▬			
2.2 Analyse customer complaints	▬▬▬	▬▬▬			
2.3 Interview staff			▬▬▬	▬▬▬	
2.4 Arrange focus group				▬▬▬	▬▬▬
2.5 Workflow analysis			▬▬▬	▬▬▬	
2.6 Interim report					▬▬▬

Figure 3.18 *Gantt chart*

Though simple, Gantt charts have an immediate impact. They are a powerful way of showing the length of time that different activities are expected to take, and which activities will be running at the same time. With the aid of the Gantt chart it is worth considering the following:

◆ Are there time overlaps in project activities that will put a strain on resources? If the project team is small and one person in it is carrying out a number of activities, you may have to revise some of the start and end dates. For example, in Figure 3.18, if the same person or people are involved in activities 2.1, 2.2 and 2.3 you may run into resource problems at the end of week two that will slow down the project. You may have to postpone the focus group or you may have to seek additional resources.

◆ The chart can also highlight periods when there is very little happening. Look at this closely too. If the activity involved mainly consists of waiting for something to happen, for example for questionnaires to be returned, it might be possible to bring other activities forward and save time on the overall timetable.

Clearly the timing of specific tasks needs to be agreed with the task owner, to make sure that he or she is available when you want them. Ask project members to let you know in good time if they are planning to book holidays during the period of the project, or if they have other work commitments that will take them away from it at other times.

Your Gantt chart will also highlight the project milestones that record the project's progress towards its final deliverables.

Activity 13
Prepare a Gantt chart

Objective

Use this activity to prepare a Gantt chart for your project.

Task

You will need to consult your Work Breakdown Structure for your project, and the network diagram if you have constructed one.

1 Build a Gantt chart for your project, showing all the key tasks, including project meetings and project milestones.

Project Management

Project title:									
Stage	Wk 1	Wk 2	Wk 3	Wk 4	Wk 5	Wk 6	Wk 7	Wk 8	Wk 9
1									
1.1									
1.2									
1.3									
2									
2.1									
2.2									
2.3									
3									
3.1									
3.2									
3.3									

Feedback

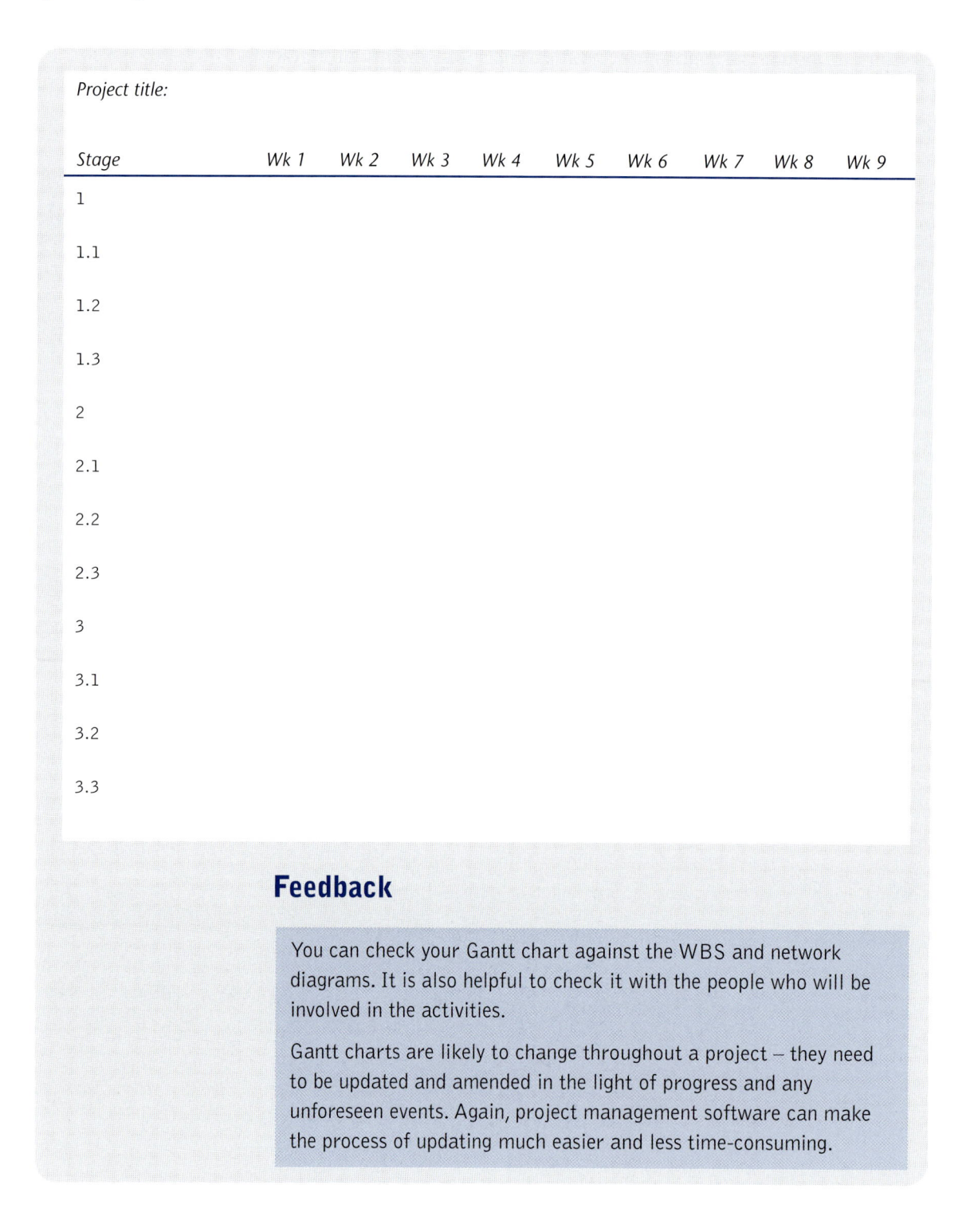

You can check your Gantt chart against the WBS and network diagrams. It is also helpful to check it with the people who will be involved in the activities.

Gantt charts are likely to change throughout a project – they need to be updated and amended in the light of progress and any unforeseen events. Again, project management software can make the process of updating much easier and less time-consuming.

Taking stock

At this point in the project – towards the end of the planning and organising stage – you're likely to have quite a collection of planning documents:

- details of your project team, customer, sponsor and other stakeholders
- a vision statement and key objectives
- scope, constraints and deliverables
- risk analysis
- WBS and task definition
- resource plan and commitment matrix
- critical path analysis
- Gantt chart.

It is essential that all the planning documents tell the same story.

This collection becomes the project's baseline documentation from which all changes have to be proposed, negotiated, recorded and agreed. By managing against this baseline documentation, the project can remain under control. The effect of any customer or project team changes can then easily be tracked, authorised and justified.

You now have all your plans in place, and are ready to take them to management for formal approval. This will not be the end of them though – plans are never set in concrete. You and your team must be prepared to review the plan regularly and make whatever adjustments are necessary.

Start-up meeting

Depending on the size and complexity of your project, as the project manager you may have a formal start-up meeting with the project sponsor, customer and perhaps other stakeholders. Alternatively you may just be given a fairly informal thumbs-up to go ahead on the basis of the project plan. Either way, you should bring your team together for an official start-up meeting. At this stage it is probably better to be over-formal than too casual. If your sponsor can come along to give a short presentation, emphasising the importance of the project to the organisation, so much the better.

This meeting fulfils a number of purposes:

- to ensure that everybody involved knows exactly what the project is and how the team will achieve its objectives
- to give the team an opportunity to ask questions, hear other people's questions, and clear up any doubts and queries
- to establish the procedures for communication and decision making, including limits on spending levels, calling project meetings, etc.

- to send them away enthused, believing in the benefits of the project and keen to start.

Don't forget, before they leave, to fix up a date for the first project review meeting, probably two to four weeks ahead.

At this stage you may find it useful to summarise the key points from the planning documentation to give to your team in a single start-up document. This will include:

- the overall vision statement
- aims and objectives
- performance indicators and targets
- activities and milestones
- a summary Gantt chart
- a list of everyone involved with the project, with their contact details – telephone and e-mail address.

◆ Recap

Review the different kinds of roles that are needed in a balanced project team

- In a really effective project team, team members should be able to cover the whole range of team roles in Belbin's classification, which he identifies as being action-oriented, people-oriented or cerebral.
- Becoming more aware of the team role(s) that you and your team members prefer to play will help you to maximise contribution and output in your team.

Identify the key activities involved in project planning

Project planning involves:

- breaking the project down into manageable units of work, known as a Work Breakdown Structure, and allocating responsibilities to individuals or groups
- producing a commitment matrix detailing the people, resources and money required for each activity
- identifying the relationships and dependencies between the activities
- identifying schedule constraints and developing a schedule.

Explore two techniques for developing and documenting project plans

- Network diagrams and Gantt charts are the most common techniques.

- A network diagram is a graphic representation of activities over time and the dependency relationships between them. There are two main types: Activity on Arrow and Activity on Node.

- A Gantt chart is easier to construct and to read than a network diagram but provides less information. Each task is represented as a bar against a project calendar; the length of the bar indicates the relative duration of each activity.

Consider how to launch the project

- The planning documents that you have assembled become the project's baseline documentation, against which you will monitor and control your project.

- A start-up meeting to formally launch the project is an effective way to motivate team members, ensure you have a common understanding about what needs to be achieved and provide an opportunity for the team to ask questions.

▶▶ More @

Mind Tools – www.mindtools.com
Visit this website for further practical guidance on how to use the project planning tools and techniques introduced in this theme.

For information on project planning software, try http://office.microsoft.com, and select Project from the list of products, or www.primavera.com. Try also www.teamflow.com – a non-traditional approach to project planning which focuses on information flow.

The Project Management Institute (PMI) – www.pmi.org
This organisation offers guidance for project planning as part of the *Project Management Body of Knowledge* available as a download from its website.

Lewis, J. (1999) *The Project Manager's Desk Reference*, McGraw-Hill
This widely acknowledged reference book provides guidance on project planning tools, including Work Breakdown Structures, PERT, CPM, and Gantt schedules.

4 Putting the plan into action

It's no accident that the bulk of this book is devoted to the aspects of initiation and planning. If you have managed these phases well, your job at this stage – putting the plan into action – should be far easier. That said, there's still plenty to do.

Firstly, you need to get your team working effectively as quickly as possible. This calls for well-developed leadership and team building skills on the part of the project manager. Then you need to keep track of what's happening. No project can run itself without careful and constant monitoring, and it's almost certain that you'll encounter change or have problems to solve at some point.

The key to managing the implementation phase is communication – from you to the various project stakeholders and from them to you. As project manager, this is a central part of your role.

This theme explores these issues further. You will:

- Assess the leadership skills that inspire high performance in a team and consider your own strengths and development needs as a project leader
- Explore techniques for building and motivating a team
- Review how to monitor and control a project
- Use techniques for recognising and solving problems.

Qualities of the project manager

The following activities are particularly important for the project manager:

- planning
- motivation
- communication
- monitoring.

Leadership can be added to this list as a general, overall need.

Planning

Many projects come to grief because the planning for them was inadequate in some way. A common fault is to spend too little time and effort on the planning stages, in a rush to get the project underway – often under pressure from senior management to deliver a solution quickly. Essential elements of the plan are overlooked or done very sketchily, in the hope that the team will muddle through or that problems can be solved as they arise. They won't. Although the different stages of the planning process may sound finicky and boring, they really are essential. Even quite small projects will benefit from, for example, a risk assessment or time spent in apportioning task responsibilities appropriately and fairly.

Along with planning goes organisation and documentation. Pull together all your key planning documents and any relevant procedures, whether existing within the organisation or devised especially for the project, that you and your team may need to refer to. Take control of the planning process, and send out a clear message of competence and authority to the project sponsor, team and other stakeholders. Note that taking control of the planning process doesn't mean that you make all the decisions without reference to anybody else: you can't reasonably plan something without consulting the person or people who will actually be responsible for achieving it, and getting their agreement and commitment.

You need to take control of the planning process, but be careful that the process doesn't take control of you. The flipside of good planning is to get so fixated on getting the complex mechanics of it right and rejigging plans and timetables that nothing much actually happens in terms of project activities.

Motivation

Projects are about change, but change cannot happen without the agreement and buy-in of the people who have to work to make it happen. The ability to encourage commitment in a team is a key skill for the project manager.

Having a motivated team, where everyone is working together and encouraging each other towards a shared goal, won't necessarily guarantee you success, but having a demotivated, unhappy and resentful team greatly increases your chances of failure and a lot of misery all round.

Maybe you already regard yourself as a motivating manager, whose own staff work enthusiastically under your leadership? Fine – that's an excellent start, but don't get complacent about it. You may find that motivating a project team can be rather different. The team might well include people you don't know, or don't like, whose involvement has been imposed on you. It could involve staff whose work on the project may be temporary or intermittent, whose energies will be directed elsewhere, and who have no real personal stake in the success or otherwise of the project. You will certainly have to be alert to, and take account of, some very varied personal agendas.

> Think about the kinds of things that motivate you: is it financial reward, the feeling of belonging to a particular group of mutually supportive people, job status, the promise of promotion or some other form of recognition from senior management? Maybe it's all of these things at different times. Remember that people's motivation needs are individual to them. They are also constantly changing and developing.

You probably won't be in a position to offer your project team members promotion or a pay rise for their efforts on your project, but somehow you will have to inspire them to deliver on target, to commit to the success of the project and to see it through to the end in spite of problems and difficulties.

The following can help.

> **Ideas for encouraging commitment from team members:**
> - Give people real responsibility for doing things and trust them to get on with it without your constant interference and/or criticism.
> - Where possible match people's interests and experience to their tasks, and try to find ways to stretch them – perhaps by applying a skill in a different way or in a different work area.
> - Make sure that people have the right skills for the task and arrange training for any shortfall.
> - Treat everyone openly, fairly and equally.
> - Work through problems with people – promptly and without offering patronising solutions.
> - Deal with problems as soon as you become aware of them. They won't go away if you shut your eyes to them. If others see you take effective action this will bolster your authority and the team's respect.
> - Acknowledge people's efforts and successes openly. Take an interest in them, and make it clear that you read the reports they send through.
> - Communicate, communicate, communicate – and keep your door open. Remember that communication is a two-way process. You need to talk to team members, but you also need to encourage them to talk to you, so that you can be

aware of any potential problems and take action to avoid them or minimise their impact.

- Make sure everyone is clear about who is doing what, and how it will be measured.

- Establish the team culture by instituting formal working procedures to cover the way the project is actually run – for example frequency and style of reporting on progress, the way project meetings are handled, the way problems are dealt with within the team, and behavioural standards, such as speed of response to requests and accessibility. Then insist everyone adheres to these rules.

- Just because you're the project manager doesn't mean you have to know it all – take the opportunity to learn from your team members.

Communication

Good communication is an essential part of motivation and effective project management but surprisingly difficult to get right.

Most of us like to think that we're good communicators. Use the following list to check your own skills in this area.

Communication checklist:
- **Clarity:** does the response and feedback you get indicate that the recipient of your message has understood it properly?
- **Appropriateness:** what's best for the purpose – a six-page report or a short e-mail with four bullet points?
- **Grapevine assumptions:** do you sometimes assume that because you've told one or two team members about something, the message will automatically get around the rest?
- **Inclusiveness:** on a fast-moving project, it is easy to overlook people who are only intermittently involved in it – but they need to be kept informed too.
- **Need to know:** the reverse of inclusiveness. Don't overload people with information they don't need.

Think about the ways in which information circulates around the project. Does the flow of information tend to be top down, with most information, (and ideas, comments and feedback) coming from you to the project team, or is the flow more circular, with all team members having an equal opportunity to contribute?

Monitoring

The basic task here is to check performance against plan, address problems that have arisen and, with your team, keep the project on track.

This assumes of course that you know exactly what is to be achieved and how you will know when it is completed. Monitoring has other aspects too – notably tuning your antennae in to potential problems that may affect the project.

Leadership

The old-fashioned view of leaders is that they are born, not made – the general riding out to glory at the head of his troops. This was great for those seen to have dash and charisma, but a bit tough on everybody else. In fact, there have been a number of schools of thought on leadership.

One of the most popular takes the view that good leaders adapt their approach to different situations depending on the individual, the team, the task and the timetable.

These approaches can range along a spectrum from the autocratic, 'you do it because I say so', at one end, to the laissez-faire, 'do whatever you think is right – that's fine by me', at the other. This doesn't rule out being inspirational as well. In fact one thing the experts do agree on is the need for flexibility in leadership style. Here are some examples of styles and when they might be appropriate:

- **Autocratic:** perhaps a crisis has arisen which needs rapid and decisive resolution, or the team leader has to intervene to resolve a dispute between team members that is threatening the cohesion of the group.
- **Seeking validation:** the team leader has formulated a decision that is presented to the group for discussion and possible change. This can work where the team is still fairly new and not confident enough to formulate its own ideas.
- **Opinion seeking:** this is a step up from the last, where the leader presents the team with a problem rather than a tentative solution, then makes a decision on the basis of comments and suggestions received.
- **Consensual or democratic:** aim for this as your everyday style. Team members fully participate in team decisions, and develop buy-in and commitment to the project.
- **Laissez-faire:** believe it or not, this is sometimes appropriate, for example when you have technical experts in the team. It does require a high degree of trust, and don't forget that

> although you can delegate authority, you can't delegate responsibility – you will carry the can for the outcome.

The trick is recognising which leadership style is appropriate in what circumstances. There are difficulties in balancing the autocratic and democratic approaches to decision making. Project leaders need to be decisive, often in the face of incomplete or even conflicting information.

Without clear decisions, clearly communicated, projects simply drift and the team loses its impetus and focus. The temptation in a very pressured project environment is for the project leader to make decisions quickly in order to appear strong and decisive, and to keep the momentum going. One result of this is that the ownership of the decision rests entirely with the leader, and is not shared by the team. On the other hand, a process of consensus building within the team can take a long time and risk timetables slipping.

Only experience will tell you which approach to use in what circumstances, but never forget that whichever approach you take, you have to carry the team with you.

There is also some debate about the characteristics of the effective team leader. Here is one version:

The effective team leader:
- is true to themselves and their beliefs
- is clear about the standards they wish to achieve
- can give and receive trust and loyalty
- maintains the integrity and position of the team
- is receptive to people's hopes, needs and dignity
- faces facts honestly
- encourages personal and team development
- establishes and maintains sound working procedures
- tries to make work a happy and rewarding place.

Source: *Woodcock* (1989)

Project Management

Activity 14
Assess your project management skills

Objective

Use this activity to test your project management skills.

Task

1 For each of the statements below, ring the number under the response that you feel is right for you when managing a project – then add up your total.

   1 = I agree

   2 = I agree most of the time

   3 = I'm not sure

   4 = I don't think I agree

   5 = I disagree completely

Statements	Response
Monitoring is key to project success	1 2 3 4 5
A project team can make or break a project	1 2 3 4 5
If you listen to people, they listen to you	1 2 3 4 5
Plans provide a strong basis for management decisions	1 2 3 4 5
Change is an opportunity to be grasped	1 2 3 4 5
Conflict can be good if managed well	1 2 3 4 5

Source: *Baguley* (1999)

Total score:

   24–30 You can't be serious!

   18–23 Some thought needed here

   12–17 Well done – a good score and a strong basis to build on

   6–12   Excellent – now go and do it!

2 On the basis of the above score, what would you say your strengths and weaknesses are as a project manager?

4 Putting the plan into action

Strengths:

Weaknesses:

3 Devise an action plan to improve any weaknesses that you have identified. For example, is there any further reading you feel you should do on this subject? Can you shadow an experienced project manager who is strong in your weaker areas? You may like to talk to your manager or mentor about action you can take.

Action	*When*

Building and motivating the team

You may be very happy with the people you've got as individual team members. You're confident that their skills complement each other, that all team roles are adequately covered and that the team members will work well together. However, you need to be aware that all teams go through a series of stages before they can become fully effective.

Building the team

Pulling a team together is no easy job – some team members will be confident, (or overconfident) while others will be unsure of how well they will perform, and there will be varying degrees of enthusiasm for the project. It is your task as project leader to get all the members working as a team as quickly as possible – able to deal rapidly and decisively with conflicts or challenges from team members.

Mike Woodcock (1989) has put together a model based on the four stages of team development – shown as a 24-hour clock in Figure 4.1. But he warns that no team ever exhibits the characteristics of one stage only – it is more a question of which characteristics are prominent at the time.

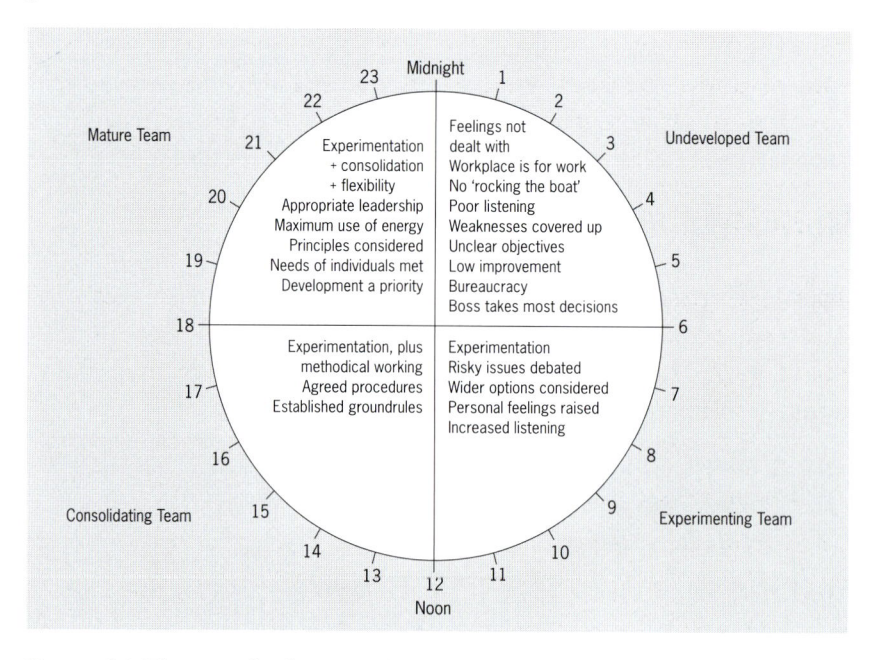

Figure 4.1 *The team development clock* Source: *Woodcock* (1989)

The clock shows four quadrants:
- **Undevelopped Team** (Midnight–6): Feelings not dealt with, Workplace is for work, No 'rocking the boat', Poor listening, Weaknesses covered up, Unclear objectives, Low improvement, Bureaucracy, Boss takes most decisions
- **Experimenting Team** (6–Noon): Experimentation, Risky issues debated, Wider options considered, Personal feelings raised, Increased listening
- **Consolidating Team** (Noon–18): Experimentation, plus methodical working, Agreed procedures, Established groundrules
- **Mature Team** (18–Midnight): Experimentation + consolidation + flexibility, Appropriate leadership, Maximum use of energy, Principles considered, Needs of individuals met, Development a priority

Stage 1 is the undeveloped team.
People have come together with a shared objective but have not had time to think about how they should work together. This is not yet a team – it's a group of individuals who have no shared understanding of what needs to be done, and who are more interested in talking

than listening. Since the group lacks the skills to support or eliminate weaknesses, these are covered up. At this stage, people will cling on to the established line – 'this is the way we do things here' – and even constructive ideas are not welcomed, while outside threats to the group are met with defensiveness.

Stage 2 is the experimenting team.
The team has decided it wants to review its operating methods and take on activities to improve its performance. Problems are faced openly, and there is an increase in real listening and understanding. More personal issues are raised, and the team starts to debate underlying values and beliefs. This can have the effect of causing some temporary feelings of insecurity in the group, or it may become so engrossed in its own problems that it rejects other groups.

Stage 3 is the consolidating team.
The team now has the confidence and mutual trust to take a hard look at its operating methods and adopt a more systematic approach – not imposed from outside as in Stage 1 but agreed within the team. Decisions are now taken in a structured way, by clarifying the purpose of the task and then working through the objectives, information gathering, considering the options, planning what needs to be done and reviewing the outcome.

In Stage 4 the team finally reaches maturity.
The keynote is flexibility, with different procedures adopted for different needs. Individuals are committed to the team's success, and with trust, openness and co-operation in place, people are less concerned with defending their positions. Figure 4.1 summarises these four stages as segments of a 24-hour clock.

Motivating the team

Team motivation is a key requirement for the project leader. Let's look now at some barriers to motivation identified by Spencer and Pruss (1992). These can be intangible or tangible barriers. Intangible barriers can include:

- lack of senior management commitment
- out-of-date working practices
- being unsure of our own power as individuals – so the team is unaware of its collective authority
- using history as an excuse for not doing things
- imagining real or imaginary power blocs that may frustrate the team's efforts.

Some of the tangible barriers are:

- social and environmental constraints
- out-of-date plant and equipment
- poor working conditions
- poor relationships – with management, staff, suppliers and customers
- not enough staff and lack of training
- time constraints
- too low a level of authorisation for resources.

How do you know if your team is demotivated? Davis et al. (1992) suggest a quick 10-point health check.

Motivation health check:
- People are often late or miss meetings unnecessarily
- Positions are entrenched so 'it's not my job' is likely to be heard
- Too much time is spent going over old ground
- Jobs are assigned to individuals, which are almost complete projects in their own right
- Too much work is changed or has to be redone after a team meeting
- One or more people at any team meeting seems to have their own hidden agenda
- People accept tasks for a team, but never get them done on time
- Deadlines are just far enough away for you not to argue with them, but there are few detailed plans
- Teams seem to produce long reports, but are short on real output
- Priorities keep being changed as problems arise.

Source: *Davis et al.* (1992)

If you can say yes to more than three of these, you need to take corrective action. With more than five you're in trouble – with a stressed team into the bargain. You can forestall some problems by taking the practical steps suggested by Spencer and Pruss (1992):

- Make team members feel valued by:
    - holding regular progress meetings
    - showing interest in whatever the team holds to be important
    - nurturing an atmosphere of approval and co-operation

- ensuring that each member understands the importance of his/her contribution
- making sure the team understands the purpose and goals of the organisation

◆ Provide scope for development:
- provide on and off-the-job training
- arrange and facilitate internal and external contacts
- use inter-team training and encourage horizontal communication
- agree sensible and achievable targets

◆ Recognise achievements:
- praise and communicate the team's success within the organisation
- report regularly to senior management and pass on their comments and praise
- hold regular sessions to look at individual progress
- communicate the company's results and achievements and how the team has contributed to these

◆ Provide challenge:
- establish and communicate the team's objectives
- enable the team to take the maximum amount of responsibility
- foster and encourage ideas and challenges.

Activity 15
Identify the stages of team development

Objective

Use this activity to understand the different development stages that all teams go through.

Task

1 Think of a team that you are a member of. Look again at the different stages of team building in the previous section:

   ◆ undeveloped
   ◆ experimenting
   ◆ consolidating
   ◆ mature.

Project Management

Identify which stage the team is currently at, providing some evidence for your assessment.

2 If the team is in one of the first three stages, what action do you think you can take to move the team forward to the next stage?

Team:

Stage the team is currently at – and evidence for this	*Action needed to move the team forward*

Feedback

If the team is still in the early stages of working together, you can help by encouraging team members to recognise each other's strengths and to work to these. The early stages of team development can be challenging – you might wonder how people who are in conflict now can ever work together harmoniously. But conflict can be creative too, provided it is used positively rather than being seen as entirely negative.

Perhaps your team is already mature? Take a second look – maybe the team has been together for so long it has lost all its impetus, and needs some active encouragement to get it revitalised and creative again.

4 Putting the plan into action

Project progress and review

Even before you get the final go-ahead on your project, you may have seen how quickly – and sometimes unexpectedly – something can happen to make you revise your project objectives or timetable. If this can happen in the planning stage, it is clearly much more important to monitor carefully what's happening when the project is underway, with real resources being used.

The monitoring process

However efficient the project manager, and however talented the project team, no project can run itself without careful and constant monitoring. This process needs to be planned early on, so that all team members and other stakeholders are clear what the monitoring and review mechanism is. In essence, the monitoring process will follow the stages shown in Figure 4.2.

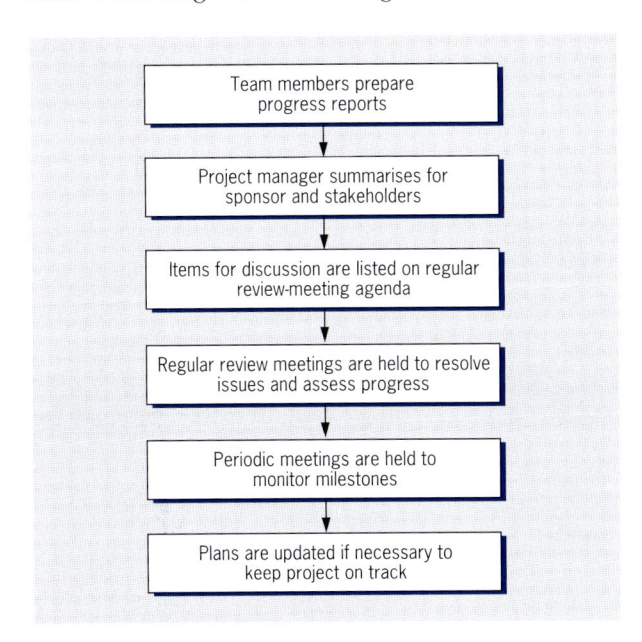

```
Team members prepare
progress reports
        ↓
Project manager summarises for
sponsor and stakeholders
        ↓
Items for discussion are listed on regular
review-meeting agenda
        ↓
Regular review meetings are held to resolve
issues and assess progress
        ↓
Periodic meetings are held to
monitor milestones
        ↓
Plans are updated if necessary to
keep project on track
```

Figure 4.2 *The monitoring process* Source: *Bruce and Langdon* (2000)

Factors that can change projects

The first thing you have to accept is that change on projects is inevitable, particularly if they involve a number of people over a lengthy period of time.

Here are some common causes of change:

- the customer changes their mind about what they want
- organisational factors such as a restructure or reshuffle of senior staff roles

> - management wishes to change the emphasis of a project, expand or contract its scope
> - some of your key team members leave
> - some of your original assumptions, for example in terms of resource requirement or risk assessment, turn out to be wrong.

Not all causes of change are bad. You may find that you need to revise the project timetable because a milestone has been reached more quickly than expected, or that the project has to be extended because the customer sees wider implications for the outcomes of the project, for example a new market opens up.

Whatever the reason for change, the necessary adjustments to the project plan need to be made as quickly as possible. The first thing to do is to bring your team together for a group discussion on the change and the impact it will or might have on the project's staffing, budget and timetable.

If it is a major change, such as a shift of focus and objectives, or is caused by the loss of one or more team members, perhaps by redundancy, you will have a major job to boost people's morale. Cynicism is very common in these situations – 'Huh! And they said it was such an important project'. People may be very ready to believe that the change reflects management's low opinion of the project or their own importance and ability.

Do deal with issues like this honestly, taking time to counsel individual staff as necessary. But you also need to act decisively, encourage the team to see change as an opportunity to review the plan, and move forward.

All changes to the plan need to be formally documented and agreed with the project sponsor and customer. Updating the baseline documentation throughout a change process is key to maintaining project visibility and control.

Reviewing and reporting progress

Effective project management involves you in constant monitoring of a whole range of things – progress against specific objectives, the rate at which resources are being consumed, how well the project team is working together, and maintaining close contact with your sponsor, customer and stakeholders. You will also need to be sensitive to what might happen, in case you need to take evasive or corrective action.

The key to all of this is good communication – from you to others, and from others to you.

4 Putting the plan into action

From you to others ...

- Hold regular team review meetings (about one a month, more often if the situation demands it) and use these as a way of developing good communications around the team. Deal with problems in an open and honest manner. Set a clear and consistent agenda (many items will be standing items, valid from one meeting to the next), and check that the action points from the previous meeting have actually been carried out. If you don't take these things seriously, neither will your team. Bruce and Langdon (2000) suggest colour coding the issues reported using red, amber or green to indicate the degree of urgency or priority.

- Hold one-to-one meetings with individual team members. People may be more open in a one-to-one situation, and you can discuss specifics in a way that's difficult in a group.

- Prepare short, regular situation reports on the project's progress for your sponsor, customer and stakeholders. Devise a standard structure or form for these under set headings so that progress can be more easily tracked over time. Manage your stakeholder relationships actively – make the most of what support you can get, and be alert to the people who may hinder you.

- Walk around and talk to people, or keep in telephone contact if they work at a distance. Gather whatever information and intelligence you can that may be of use to your project – it may help you to see your way through a problem or shorten the time needed to reach a milestone.

From others to you ...

- The best way of keeping in touch with progress is for your team members to report in regularly on their own tasks. Make clear the kind of information you want and how often you need it. Do show a genuine interest in this. Ask questions if you're not clear about something, congratulate them on progress made or difficulties successfully resolved, and be alert to danger signs, for example late reports, hurriedly cobbled together with little or no attempt to quantify progress, from a team member who never seems to be around when you want to contact them.

- Encourage feedback from your sponsor, customer and stakeholders. It is demoralising and insulting to your and the team's efforts to have your reports received without comment. Silence can hide both general satisfaction and dissatisfaction – you need the reassurance from them that the project is on track in terms of their expectations.

Project Management

Using the 'S' curve for monitoring

A simple way to monitor the benefits gained as project monies are spent is to use the 'S' curve representation. See Figure 4.3. Here expenditure, or cost, is plotted against time and compared to the forecasted budget expenditure. A measure of value due to project effort is also added. The figure for value added can be either in terms of contractual monies paid for delivery against agreed milestones, sometimes called progress payments, or for an internal project a financial measure that shows how the project is improving performance of the service or product. Some ingenuity may be required in order to come up with such a figure but any figure is better than simply waiting until the project is completed before evaluating the benefit or value added by it.

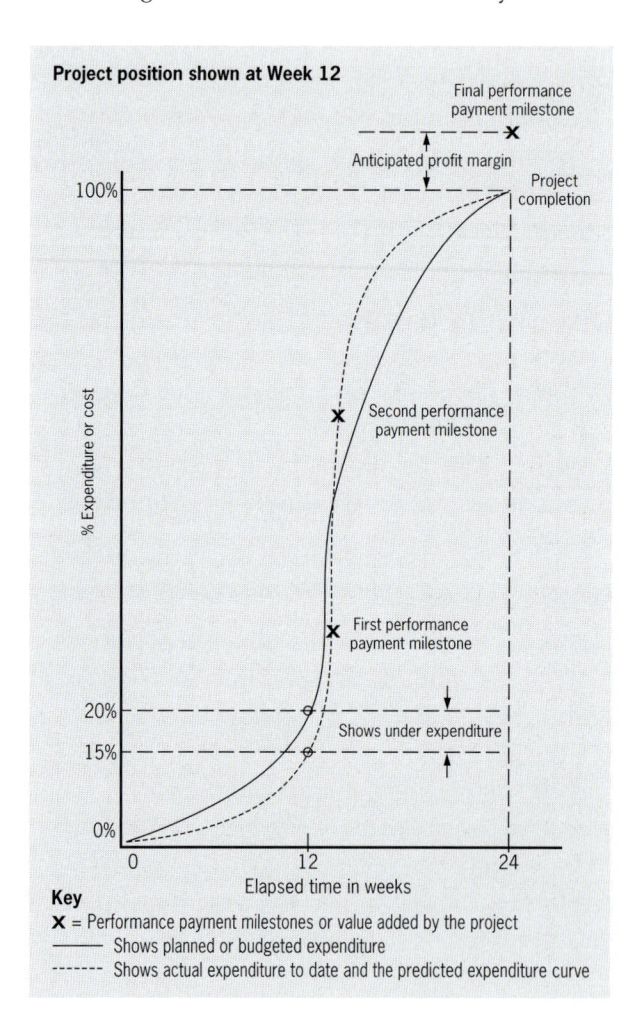

Figure 4.3 *The project 'S' curve representation*

Figure 4.3 shows that project expenditure has been lower than planned, which is probably due to a late start on the project. This is a common occurrence when the team finds that picking up momentum is difficult because the project definition and responsibilities have not been fully understood before the project launch. This means that a high rate of expenditure is now required in order to meet the first performance payment milestone which is due in week 13. People will be working overtime and the pressure will be on to get purchase orders approved and equipment ordered.

You may at first be surprised that an underspend is seen as a harbinger of bad news. But the new predicted rate of expenditure required to get the project done and meet the payment milestones will have serious implications for both project cash flow and the demand on resources.

A network diagram should also be used in conjunction with this 'S' curve representation to investigate options for taking a different approach to tackling the project. Pressing ahead with an underspend, or even trying to recover from an overspend, by simply working harder to deliver to the original plan, is often a hallmark of poor project management. Plans are only indicators of your original thinking and as a project progresses the new insight that this brings should be used to revise old plans.

We are not advocating change for change's sake but that planning myopia can be minimised by being prepared to challenge status quo thinking. This is known as applying the vigorous project management approach.

Managing information and learning

As part of the project planning process, you may have used information recycled from another project, perhaps statistical or survey data, or guidance on performance indicators and targets. Your project will also generate information that is potentially useful to other people, for example:

- Project planning data: current or earlier versions of project plans, contacts data, agendas and action checklists from review meetings and project reports. These will need to be accessible to project team members and other interested parties, and should be arranged in a way that provides a see-at-a-glance view of progress.
- Other useful information such as market studies, analyses and assessments by team members and others, proposed new business models and industry benchmarks, etc.

On complex projects, where everyone is busy with their own responsibilities, it can be difficult to ensure that the project's information resource is managed efficiently and kept up to date. This is most easily done by giving responsibility for it to one person who will undertake to arrange it in a sensible order and provide an index.

Dealing with problems

The best laid plans and projects will encounter some difficulties sooner or later.

Problem identification

If you are very alert, with an experienced project team, you may be able to see potential problems developing and forestall them before they do any damage. Contact your team members regularly to check progress, and encourage them to report problems to you at the earliest possible stage, and if it's something serious, make sure that you are the first to know. There are few things more undermining to a project manager's credibility than discovering that a problem, which has been simmering away unknown to them, is about to explode into a major crisis.

There are various stages in effectively managing problems:

- agree what the problem is
- identify the possible causes
- generate options for resolving the problem
- assess the options and select an appropriate one
- implement a solution, and review it.

We will start by looking at problem identification.

One useful tool for identifying the causes of problems is a fishbone diagram – so called because in outline it looks like the skeleton of a fish. It is also known as a cause and effect diagram, because what it does is provide a systematic way of looking at effects – what is actually happening – and the causes which are giving rise to these effects or contributing to them.

It can be used where a problem has been identified, where things are beginning to go wrong and it's not clear why, or where the results of a process or activity have been very different from those anticipated.

Here are the stages in constructing a fishbone diagram:

1 First of all, define the problem for which the causes must be identified, for example packages delivered late.

2 Draw a thick horizontal arrow, which represents the spine of the fish, and point it to the right. Label the arrow-head with the problem.

3 Brainstorm the major categories of possible causes. Some typical examples are:

- the four Ms: Methods, Machines, Materials, Manpower

- the four Ps: Place, Procedures, People, Provisions
- the four Ss: Surroundings, Suppliers, Systems, Skills

4   Draw arrows for each of these main categories, pointed in towards the spine at an angle of about 70 degrees.

5   For each main category, brainstorm the specific causes, and add them to the diagram as subsidiary arrows.

6   Repeat the procedure for as long as you get useful answers.

7   Once all the bones have been added, identify the likely root cause.

Figure 4.4 is a worked example that should make the process clearer.

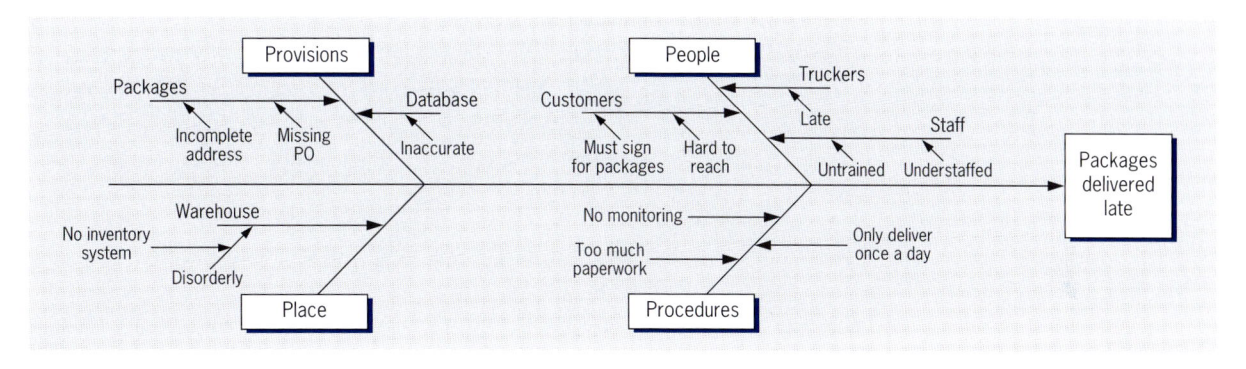

Figure 4.4 *Fishbone diagram*   Source: *MIT* (1996)

> **Constructing a fishbone diagram – tips for making sure that the process is successful:**
>
> ◆ Make sure that everybody is agreed on what the problem or effect is.
>
> ◆ Make sure that you are stating causes not solutions.
>
> ◆ Don't try to solve problems that are outside the group's experience or control.
>
> ◆ Pay particular attention to causes that appear repeatedly, and examine which causes would repay further investigation.
>
> ◆ Reach a team consensus. If you have identified more causes than you can comfortably handle, team members can vote on the most likely ones.
>
> ◆ Test the most likely cause and verify.

Source: *MIT* (1996)

With experience, you and your team will learn to identify both the minor problems and the ones that will have a major impact on the project if they are not addressed immediately.

For example, if your problem is with a supplier that consistently promises and fails to meet delivery times, it is unlikely to change of its own accord. Check the contract – are there penalties you can impose, or is there some leeway to switch suppliers?

Make use of all the help you can get from your team members and stakeholders who may be more experienced than you at handling this kind of problem.

If the problem involves personality clashes within the team, you will need to deal with it quickly and assertively, talking to the people concerned and brokering a positive and peaceful outcome.

Problem-solving techniques

Although project tasks are set out in a linear sequence – start at A and end at B – much of the monitoring and review process is iterative and cyclical: it doubles back on itself, reviews an action or problem and then moves forward.

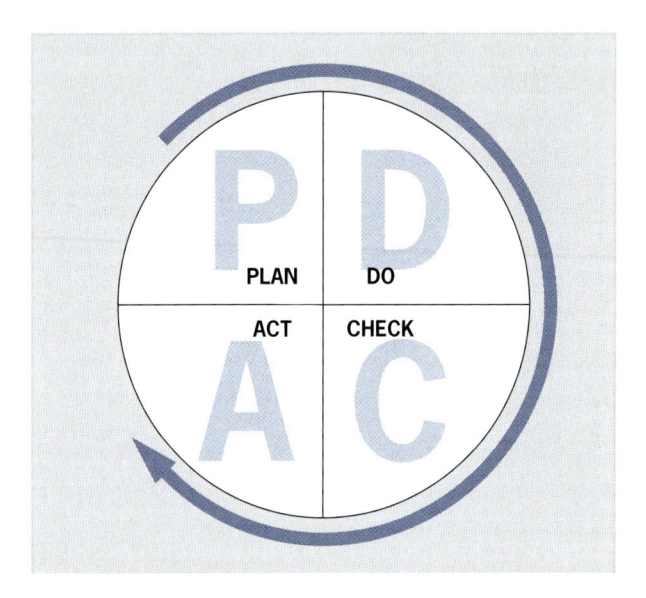

Figure 4.5 *The PDCA cycle* Source: *Adapted from HCi* (www)

One useful model of this 'problem faced to problem solved' cycle is the Plan–Do–Check–Act or PDCA cycle. This was developed in the 1930s as a tool in continuous improvement, and stresses the cyclical nature of improvement programmes, beginning with planning and resulting in effective action. This is what each stage of the cycle involves:

Plan: find out which things are going wrong and come up with ideas for solving the problems.

Do: implement changes designed to solve the problems on a small or experimental scale first. This minimises disruption to routine, whether the changes work or not.

Check: whether these changes are achieving the desired result.

Act: to implement changes on a larger scale if the experiment is successful. Also act to involve other people, for example your project stakeholders who are affected by the changes and whose co-operation you need to implement them on a larger scale, or those who may simply benefit from what you have learned.

If the experiment was not successful, skip the Act stage and go back to Plan to come up with some fresh ideas for solving the problem and go through the cycle again.

If the problem is a complex one, it may benefit from using some formal problem-solving techniques at the Plan stage. Mcdonald (1999) suggests nine steps to help you make a decision when faced with a problem:

1. Be clear what the problem is – check the facts before reacting.
2. Is the problem unique? If not, see if what was decided before would work now.
3. Does the problem require just one (right or wrong) decision, or is it a matter of choosing the best of several options?
4. Consider a group brainstorming session: even an off-the-wall idea might spark off a useful line of thought.
5. Consult someone who has had experience of the same problem.
6. Make sure you have enough information to make a proper decision.
7. Apply a critical path analysis to each option and weed out those that are not acceptable.
8. Make sure that your information is reliable and up to date – the person who gathered it may have lacked experience, time, or based their research on false assumptions.
9. When necessary, postpone a decision to give you space to clarify your thoughts.

Six Thinking Hats technique

We may feel that many heads are better than one, but in practice find group discussions frustrating and confusing. People approach a problem from different directions, take opposing positions, argue and talk at cross-purposes. Somehow the discussion moves on, and a decision is made, but people are often left with a sense of unease. Were all the aspects of a problem explored fully? Is the decision the right one?

The Six Thinking Hats technique, developed by Edward de Bono (1985), is a simple way of slowing down thinking and making it explicit. It is based on the idea that there are six distinct categories of thinking – such as being creative and being judgemental – and that thinking is most constructive if group members are able to focus all thinking energies on one category of thinking at a time. The six categories of thinking are each represented by a metaphorical coloured hat.

In a group the technique depends on everyone playing the game. Participants agree that when they all mentally put on a particular coloured hat, they will all use that colour's category of thinking. This encourages people to think in parallel, rather than in a confrontational way.

The Six Thinking Hats are as follows:

The white hat	facts and information known or needed
The black hat	logical, judgemental and cautious – why an idea or a proposal may not work
The yellow hat	positive, optimistic and logical – why an idea will work and the benefits it brings
The red hat	feelings, emotions, intuitions – without having to justify them
The green hat	creativity, possibilities, options, new ideas
The blue hat	thinking about the process that is underway

The colour of the hat gives a direction to the discussion. Of course the direction of the discussion can be switched. 'That's good white hat thinking. Let's do some green hat thinking for a while,' means that having focused on the information that participants can bring to the discussion, they symbolically take off the white hat, put on the green hat and start to generate new ideas.

De Bono argues that Six Hats thinking can make meetings more productive and save time. It helps everyone to combine their knowledge, intelligence and expertise and work together.

Nominal group technique

Another more formal approach to problem solving is the nominal group technique. This involves all the members of a group and uses consensus to evaluate and rank all the ideas generated. It is very democratic, as its outcome is a group agreement about what action is required to solve the problem. Here are the steps:

1. The team leader presents the problem (or opportunity!) to the group, without suggesting a preferred solution.
2. Working on their own, everyone writes down a list of potential solutions.
3. Everyone, in turn, reports just one of their ideas. This is recorded on a flip chart. The name of the person suggesting it is not recorded, and no comments are made about it.
4. The group has a brief discussion – ideas are clarified, and similar ones amalgamated, provided their owners agree.
5. Each member of the group, working on their own, identifies their 'top 5' ideas in order of preference, and gives it to the group leader without sharing it within the group.
6. The leader generates a 'top 5' group list from the individual lists. This is reported back to the group and discussed. Finally, a vote is taken to identify the idea(s) to be actioned.

Source: *Baguley* (1999)

4 Putting the plan into action

Activity 16
Explore the nominal group technique

Objective

Use this activity to explore the nominal group technique as a problem-solving technique.

Task

1. Find an opportunity to use the nominal group technique to resolve a problem within a team of which you are a member. Regardless of your normal position in the team, it will be useful if you take the lead role for this activity.

2. Work through the stages of the nominal group technique to arrive at your top five solutions for discussion and voting.

3. After the exercise, ask your colleagues for feedback on how well the technique worked.

Top five solutions:

-
-
-
-
-

Colleagues feedback:

◆ Recap

Assess the leadership skills that inspire high performance in a team and consider your own strengths and development needs as a project leader

- Project managers need a broad range of skills, most notably planning, motivation, communication and monitoring.

- They need to be able to adapt their leadership approach, ranging from autocratic through to a laissez faire attitude, to meet the requirements of the different situations that they meet.

Explore techniques for building and motivating a team

- Project managers need to be skilled team builders, able to develop fully effective teams as quickly as possible. New project teams pass through four stages in their development. They are undeveloped when they first form and move through phases of experimentation and consolidation before becoming fully mature and effective.

- Spencer and Pruss suggest four approaches for motivating team members: making them feel valued, providing scope for development, recognising achievements and providing challenge.

Review how to monitor and control a project

- Once the project is underway, a monitoring process is essential to collate progress information from team members so that it can be compared against plans, corrective action can be taken and the project documentation can be kept up to date.

- The key to monitoring is effective communication. Develop communication channels and forums that support communication from you, the project manager, to your team and from them to you.

Use techniques for recognising and solving problems

- Problem solving involves:
    - agreeing what the problem is
    - identifying the possible causes
    - generating options for resolving the problem
    - assessing the options and selecting an appropriate one
    - implementing the solution and reviewing it.

- Many tools and techniques have been developed to support problem solving. Some, like fishbone diagrams, focus on identifying the root cause of the problem whereas others, such as Six Thinking Hats and the nominal group technique, encourage creative thinking when generating and assessing options.

◆ The Plan–Do–Check–Act cycle provides a framework for problem solving, beginning with planning and resulting in effective action.

▶▶ More @

Mind Tools – www.mindtools.com
This website has practical guidance sections dedicated to communication and problem-solving tools and techniques.

Belbin Associates – www.belbin.com
Visit this website for more on team roles.

***Team Building and Leading* and *Results Management* (2004)** are further books from this series that will help you to develop your team-building and leadership skills.

Briner, W., Hastings, C. and Geddes, M. (1997), *Project Leadership*, **Gower Publishing**
This is a practical book, focusing on the people aspects of project management: the underlying dynamics of the project team, the interactions between the project team and managing the project stakeholders.

Dixon, A. (2003) *The Management Task*, **Butterworth-Heinemann**
This is a comprehensive, general text for people who want to develop their managements skills.

Jones, A. (1999) *Team-building Activities for Every Group*, **Rec Room Publishing Inc**
Try team-building activities to help your team members learn more about each other in a creative way.

5 Project completion

All projects, by their definition, must come to an end and managing the final phase is just as important as starting up.

In this final theme you will:

- ◆ Explore what is involved in project closure
- ◆ Consider how you can evaluate and capture learning from your project.

Project completion, sign off and review

Managing this challenging, final phase of the project involves maintaining momentum within the project team, evaluating the project and writing the final report. It also includes organising the project documentation to capture the lessons that have been learned.

Maintaining interest

On long projects, it can be very difficult to keep the team energised and motivated, particularly as the end draws near. The short-term specialist team members will have come and gone, and members of the core team may begin to drop out, to take up new projects or go back to their normal everyday jobs. The project manager too may feel tired and demotivated, particularly if the project has been a challenging one with many problems or changes.

You might need to work quite hard to generate continued enthusiasm, focusing the team on what it has achieved and the need to complete the project in the same professional way they have carried it out so far.

It is important at this stage to stick to your established procedures and timetable, and not to let things drift and just fizzle out. Your project deserves better. Set a date for a final project meeting, when your sponsor can confirm that the project deliverables have met expectations and thank the team formally for their efforts. Your team can then disband on an upbeat note, with a real sense of achievement and the knowledge that their efforts have been recognised by people other than the project manager.

This kind of closure is easy to disregard when everyone is busy and preoccupied with other things, but has an important psychological effect that will colour their attitudes to working with you – or each other – again.

Project closure and evaluation

As the project manager, it will be your job to bring the project to its formal close by checking that all necessary procedures have been properly carried out and that there are no loose ends. Sometime in the future, when the project's effects can be more clearly seen, it may be useful to carry out at least one review of impact. For now, the initial review is to enable a clean sign off for the project by its sponsors and customers.

> **Sign off checklist:**
> - Has the project met all its objectives?
> - What are its specific results and benefits?
> - Is there anything that has not been achieved?
> - Are the reasons for this clearly understood and documented?
> - Have all costs been accounted for?
> - Have all project-specific resources been re-assigned?
> - Are there outstanding issues that still need resolution?
> - What learning has taken place on the project? Has this been recorded for future use?

The project report

Throughout any project, you will prepare progress reports, situation reports and perhaps interim reports at crucial stages in the project's life cycle. If the outcome of the project is to produce something concrete, such as a prototype, a piece of software or a new product, you may wonder why a report is necessary at all. However, project final reports can have two main functions:

> - to persuade management to adopt a particular plan of action in accordance with your recommendations
> - to place on record what has actually been done and achieved.

The report structure will vary according to its purpose. If the project has been set up to investigate a particular problem, you will probably find it helpful to structure it as follows.

> **Suggested report structure:**
> - Executive summary – a summary highlighting the main points and recommendations
> - Introduction – the background to the project, what the problem was

Project Management

> - Methodology – techniques for gathering relevant data
> - Findings – key issues emerging from the data gathered, and options for their resolution
> - Recommendations – the next steps
> - Appendices – project personnel, staff interviewed, copy of questionnaire used, Gantt chart and other supporting documentation.

If your project has had a concrete output, it will still be valuable to record your progress towards it, though the report will be set out in a different way – perhaps describing the particular chronological stages that the project passed through, or a department-by-department description of activities.

The aim is for the reader to be able to follow the progress of the project clearly and easily. Whatever format you use, you must make sure that all the project's aims and objectives are adequately covered. Agree with your sponsor the distribution of the report: who will receive just the executive summary and who will get the full report.

Learning from the project

Over time, your project will have generated a lot of information that may be of value to other projects or as part of individual and group learning. Putting this information in a form where others can access it can save precious time on other projects. It can also provide benchmarks against which similar work in the future can be measured.

The question is always 'what's really worth keeping?' It is always easier to save everything than do a proper sift through a pile of documentation, but some effort now will make the resource very much more valuable – and you know if you don't do it now, it will never get done. Here are some of the possibilities for you to discuss and agree with your team:

> - copies of any templates produced – for the project plan, interviews, questionnaires, updated report forms, etc.
> - how the project was managed
> - financial information and reporting
> - performance against target
> - the project's critical success factors
> - skills gaps and the action taken to fill them
> - what went well and what didn't, and what would be done differently next time

5 Project completion

- unplanned events and their impact
- team learning from the project.

With all this recorded for future use, your project will have an influence, and possible impact, well beyond its original parameters.

Activity 17
Analyse strengths and weaknesses of a project

Objective

Use this activity to assess a project's strengths and weaknesses.

Task

1 Identify a recent project in which you have been involved or which affected you in some way. You may like to revisit the project you have used for earlier activities.

2 Arrange to meet the manager of this project. Talk through with them its strengths and weaknesses, what they think went well and what didn't (and why) and see what you can learn from their experiences. Note the key points below:

Strengths	Weaknesses

3 Establish whether any learning from the project was formally captured for future use. If yes – what was it, and how has it been preserved? If no – what could have been usefully recorded for later project managers?

Project Management

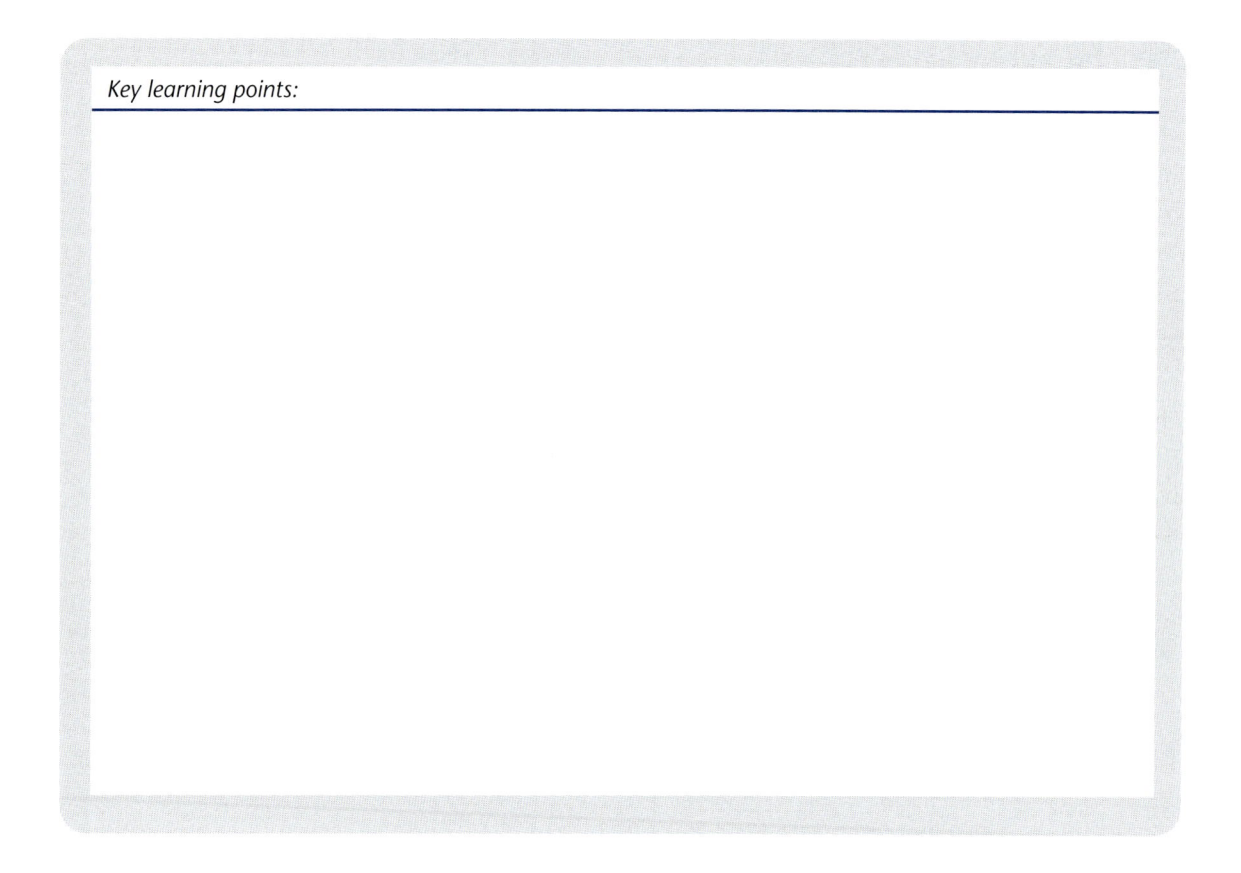

> Key learning points:

◆ Recap

Explore what is involved in project closure

It can be difficult to maintain momentum at the end of a project but two activities are particularly important:

- ◆ Gaining signoff from the project sponsors and customers to agree the project has achieved its objectives, acknowledge reasons for any areas where it has been unsuccessful and account fully for all costs and resources.

- ◆ Capturing learning from the project so that it can be applied to future projects.

Consider how you can evaluate and capture learning from your project

- ◆ Consult with your team, project sponsor and customers when you are reviewing the strengths and weaknesses of your project – they are all valuable sources of information.

5 Project completion

▶▶ More @

Phillips, J., Bothell, T. and Snead, L. (2002) *Measuring the Success of Project Management Solutions,* **Butterworth-Heinemann**
Drawing on their expertise in developing and implementing return on investment (ROI) programmes in human performance and training, the authors demonstrate how you can effectively apply ROI to project management.

The Project Management Institute (PMI) – www.pmi.org
This organisation offers guidance for project completion and evaluation as part of the *Project Management Body of Knowledge,* available as a download from its website.

References

Baguley. P. (1999) *Project management,* Hodder

Belbin, M. 'Team roles', www.belbin.com/belbin-team-roles.htm

Briner, W., Hastings, C. and Geddes, M. (1997), *Project Leadership,* Gower Publishing

Brown. M., (2002) *Successful project management in a week,* Hodder

Bruce, A. and Langdon, K. (2000) *Project management,* Dorling Kindersley

Campbell, S. (1995) *From Chaos to Confidence: Survival Strategies for the New Workplace,* Simon & Schuster

Covey, S. R. (1992) *The Seven Habits of Highly Effective People,* Simon & Schuster

Davis, J., Milburn, P., Murphy, T. and Woodhouse, M. (1992) *Successful Team Building,* Kogan Page

de Bono, E. (1985) *Sex Thinking Hats,* Little, Brown and Company

HCi, www.hci.com.au/hcisite2/toolkit/pdcacycl.htm

Lake, C. (1997) *Mastering project management: key skills in ensuring profitable and successful projects,* Thorogood

Lockyer, K. and Gordon, J. (1996) 6th edition, *Project management and project network techniques,* Prentice Hall

Mcdonald, J. (1999) *Project management,* Croner

MIT (Massachusetts Institute of Technology) (1996) 'TQM: cause/effect diagram (fishbone)', http://web.mit.edu/tqm/cause_effect.html

Spencer, J. and Pruss, A (1992), *Managing your Team,* Piatkus

Woodcock, M. (1989) 2nd edition, *Team development manual,* Gower Publishing